METALLIC
Seed Bead Splendor

Nancy Zellers

Dedication

As always, my deepest thanks and gratitude to Steve and Carol for their many hours of support and criticism. Who can write a book without the help of friends?

Kalmbach Books
21027 Crossroads Circle
Waukesha, Wisconsin 53186
www.Kalmbach.com/Books

Illustrations by the author. Photography by Kalmbach Books. The designs in *Metallic Seed Bead Splendor* are copyrighted. Please use them for your education and personal enjoyment only. They may not be taught or sold without permission.

Published in 2013
17 16 15 14 13   1 2 3 4 5

Manufactured in the United States of America

ISBN: 978-0-87116-484-1

Editor: Erica Swanson
Art Director: Lisa Bergman
Layout: Tom Ford
Photographer: James Forbes

Library of Congress Cataloging-In-Publication Data
Zellers, Nancy.
    Metallic seed bead splendor : [stitch 29 timeless jewelry pieces in gold, bronze, and pewter] / Nancy Zellers.

        p. : col. ill. ; cm.

    ISBN: 978-0-87116-484-1

    1. Beadwork—Patterns. 2. Beadwork—Handbooks, manuals, etc. 3. Jewelry making—Handbooks, manuals, etc. I. Title.

TT860 .Z46 2013
745.594/2

CONTENTS

Introduction 4
A Word about Metallic Beads 5

PROJECTS

Key to My Heart Necklace 8
Rubies and Pearls Bracelet and Earrings 10
Lavish Leaf Lariat and Earrings 14
Golden Twist Necklace and Bracelet 16
Opposites Attract Bracelet 19
St. Petersburg Choker and Earrings 22
Old Coins Necklace 24
Triple St. Petersburg Bracelet 26
Gold Lace Cuff 29
Triangle Meet Cube Bracelet 32
Summer Lace Necklace and Earrings 34
Bugle Boy Bands Bracelet 36
Diabolo Necklace 38
Going Baroque with Pearls Bracelet 41
Crystal Lattice Bracelet and Earrings 44
Golden Gumdrops Necklace 48
It's a Stitch Bracelet 50
Russian Splendor Necklace 52
Twisted Herringbone Necklace 55
Caged Crystals Bracelet 58
Crowned Pendant 62
Jeweled Rings Necklace and Earrings 65
Dragon Pearls Necklace and Earrings 68
Tsarina Necklaces and Earrings 71
Metallini Cellini Bracelet 74
Captured Pearls Bracelet 76
Oval Chain Link Bracelet 78
Damascene Floral Bracelet and Earrings 80
Etruscan Necklace and Earrings 82

BASICS

Tools for Beading 88
Stitch Basics 89

About the Author 95

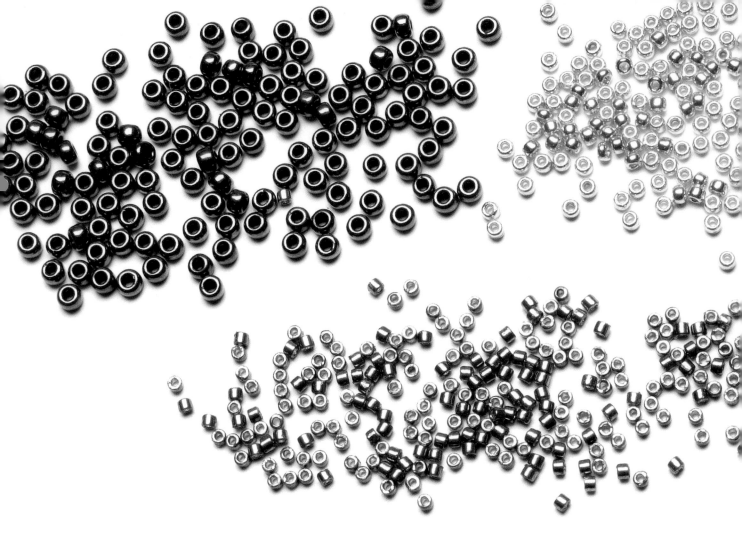

INTRODUCTION

I love the look of fine metal jewelry! It's both beautiful and versatile, as it can be casual everyday jewelry or as glamourous and high-style as anything in the jewelry world. One of my first beading projects was a 24-kt gold cylinder bead amulet bag designed by Carol Wilcox Wells—so I was attracted to the rich, shiny look of gold from the very beginning. The love affair has only continued through the years with many jewelry and sculptural pieces designed around gold beads.

This book contains some of those pieces, along with many new ones. I've also included the beautiful bronze and steel colors available in the bead-ing palette, and you can use pewter as well. A few pieces have rich accents of

crystals or pearls, and some feature the dramatic contrast between black and gold.

For most of the projects, I use seed beads, particularly those with the new permanent finishes from the Japanese manufacturers. Please note that cylinder beads and seed beads have different shapes and can't be substituted easily for each other. While Japanese seed beads and Czech seed beads are more similar in size, they sometimes have proportional differences so they don't blend easily. All this is to say: Choose your beads carefully so they work well together.

I use mostly gold beads, along with various shades of bronze in these projects (another favorite of mine is

steel). If you prefer silver to gold, feel free to change the color schemes. You can even go outside the metallic family and use any color you fancy to fit your style.

In addition to beautiful beads, you will explore many different stitches in this book. Some of them are familiar; others may be new to you. Often, you can use just the diagrams or just the text to make the pieces. For some projects, you will need to use the text to supplement the diagrams and vice versa. In some diagrams, you will find a blue star to indicate the start of the thread path for that instruction step. And if you are unfamiliar with a stitch, turn to p. 89 for stitch basics.

Have fun and Happy Beading!

A WORD ABOUT METALLIC BEADS

Gold beads come in many shades and tints, from very delicate and pale tints to deep, dark, rich colors, with stops along the way at white gold, rose golds, and green golds. The various finishes on beads add another layer of variety, ranging from solid opaques, silver-lined, and transparent, some with aurora borealis, matte, and semi-matte finishes added. Some are actually metal with or without a coating; some metal beads are solid, and some are hollow. With a bit of searching, you can find a shade of gold and a finish that will satisfy your taste.

Some gold beads have color as an integral part of the bead, like transparent glass beads or real metal beads. Other glass beads may have a finish on the exterior or may be galvanized with a metal-like coating. Silver-lined beads may be a gold-colored bead with silver-lining, or perhaps a clear bead with a gold-tinted lining. In the past, metallic beads could be a problem when the metallic finishes were not stable or flaked off easily. Today, the high-quality beads from Toho (Permanent Finish), Miyuki (Duracoat), and some Czech manufacturers rarely flake.

I have not had problems with the beads I've used in the past few years; however, your mileage may vary. If in doubt, you may want to test the beads before starting a project: Soak a few beads overnight in white vinegar or in acetone (nail polish remover) to see if the color leaches out or if the finish changes. Rubbing the beads briskly between your hands or on a hard surface can test for damage to the finish or flaking. If you have skin with high acidity, you may want to take extra precautions when wearing your beadwork. If you aren't sure about your skin type, soak a few beads in your saliva for a couple of minutes and then rub them briskly between your hands to see if the color changes.

The reflective nature of shiny gold beads can be hard on your eyes. Be sure to work in good light and take lots of breaks.

PROJECTS

KEY TO MY HEART
Necklace

Make this easy, fun necklace in three metallic colors with matching lock, key, and heart charms.

MATERIALS

Necklace, 22 in. (56cm) including clasp

15 grams 11º bronze seed beads

15 grams 11º gold seed beads

15 grams 11º silver seed beads

3 charms, one each in gold, silver, bronze

3 6mm gold jump rings

6mm silver jump ring

6mm bronze jump ring

2 6mm gold split rings

1 yd. (.9m) 2mm satin rattail cord

Beading thread

Toggle clasp

Needle

Scissors

2 pairs of chainnose pliers

STITCHES

Odd-count tubular peyote, p. 90

Zipping up, p. 90

NECKLACE

Make the Necklace Rope

1 On a comfortable length of thread (about 1–2 yd./.9–1.8m), begin odd-count peyote stitch: Pick up two 11º silver seed beads, two 11º gold seed beads, two 11º bronze seed beads, two 11º silvers, two 11º golds, and an 11º bronze. Tie the beads into a circle, leaving an 8-in. (20cm) tail. Sew through the first 11º silver picked up.

2 Picking up the same type of bead that you are exiting each time, work in odd-count tubular peyote for 21 in. (53cm). After the first inch or so, place the rope around the rattail cord.

3 Sew through the rope and rattail once or twice to secure the rattail inside the rope. Trim the rattail even with the end of the rope.

4 Pass through all the up-beads on the end of the rope, pulling them together firmly. Repeat to reinforce.

5 Sew a split ring to one end of the necklace. Using a jump ring, attach half of the clasp to the end of the necklace.

6 Repeat steps 3–5 on the other end.

Make Charm Rings

7 On a comfortable length of thread, begin odd-count tubular peyote stitch: Pick up nine 11º golds. Tie the 11º golds into a circle.

8 Work odd-count tubular peyote for 2¼ in. (5.7cm) around a piece of rattail.

9 Trim the rattail to the length of the beadwork.

10 Zip the ends together, matching the zig-zag of the beads, to make a circle of beads. It will not match perfectly, due to the odd-count spiral. Reinforce the join, and end the thread.

11 Repeat steps 7–10 with 11º silvers for 2½ in. (6.4cm).

12 Repeat steps 7–10 with 11º bronzes for 2¾ in. (7cm).

13 String a charm on a matching jump ring, and close the jump ring. Sew the jump ring to the matching bead circle near the join.

14 String the completed bead circle charms on the necklace in order from smallest to largest.

RUBIES & PEARLS
Bracelet and Earrings

Pearls, rubies, and gold
are a dramatic and
luxurious combination.

MATERIALS

Bracelet, 8½ in. (21.6cm)

8 12x12x5mm pearls

8 grams 11º gold seed beads

3 grams 11º silver-lined red seed beads

2 grams 15º gold seed beads

14 3mm silver-lined gold cube beads

2 5–6mm gold split rings

2 5–6mm gold jump rings

Toggle clasp

Earrings, 1½ in. (3.8cm)

2 12x12x5mm pearls

2 8 or 9mm coin pearl disks

1 gram 15º gold seed beads

2 grams 11º gold seed beads

2 grams 11º silver-lined red seed beads

2 4–5mm gold jump rings

Pair of gold earring posts with loop

G-S Hypo Cement (optional)

Both

Beading thread

Needle

Scissors

Clear double-sided tape

2 pairs of chainnose pliers

STITCHES

Even-count tubular peyote stitch, p. 90

Ladder stitch, p. 90

Flat right-angle weave, p. 92

> The pearls will be irregular, so the completed beads will also be slightly irregular in shape.

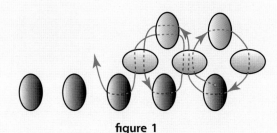

figure 1

BRACELET

Make the Bottom

1 On a comfortable length of thread, pick up four 11º gold seed beads. Tie the beads into a circle. Work a flat right-angle weave strip five stitches wide and five stitches long. Finish the last stitch by exiting the bottom bead as if you were starting a new row.

Make Side Walls

2 Stitch in right-angle weave around the outside edge: Pick up an 11º gold, an 11º red seed bead, and an 11º gold. Sew back through the original 11º gold exited and the first gold 11º picked up. Push the stitch upward so it forms a perpendicular wall to the strip. Continue in right-angle weave, picking up 11ºs each time, so an 11º red is the top bead of the stitch **(figure 1)**.

3 To turn the corner at the end of the row, exit the last side 11º picked up. Pick up an 11º red and an 11º gold. Sew through the bead of the first stitch of the bottom on the next side, the bead you exited at the start of this step, the beads picked up, and the bead on the next

row of the strip. Continue alternating the direction of each stitch.

4 Continue working in right-angle weave around the strip. Each stitch will need an 11º red and an 11º gold, except the last stitch. which will need only an 11º red to finish. Each side will have five 11º reds.

5 Stitch an 11º red between each 11º red. Pull the stitches snug. This converts the right angle weave to even-count tubular peyote. This round has 20 beads. Step up at the end of the round.

6 Cut a small piece of double-sided tape. Place it on the back of a 12x12x5mm pearl. Center the pearl in the beadwork from step 5.

Make the Top Enclosure Rows

7 Sew a 15º gold seed bead between each 11º red, and pull snug. Step up at the end of the round.

8 Sew a 15º between each 15º picked up, and pull snug. Step up at the end of the round.

Seed beads are sized by measuring across the hole. Nearly all beads of a given size are the same diameter. However, the thickness of the bead (through the hole) may vary. Japanese seed beads tend to be larger and more regular in size than Czech seed beads, many of which are quite narrow. I used Czech silver-lined red seed beads for this project, which helped when forming the bezel.

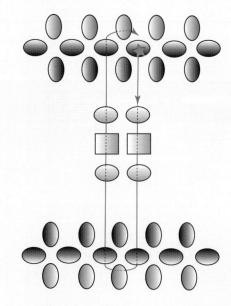

figure 2

9 Sew through all the up-beads, pulling them together snugly. Repeat to reinforce and tighten. End the thread.

10 Repeat steps 1–9 seven times for a total of eight pearl components.

Finish the Bracelet

11 Attach a thread to one of the pearl components, exiting one of the two center 11º golds in one side wall. These are the side beads of the right-angle weave strip in steps 2 and 3, which are located just below the row of 11º reds.

12 Pick up an 11º gold, a 3mm silver-lined gold cube bead, and an 11º gold. Sew through the matching center bead on another pearl component, making a bridge between the two components.

13 Sew through the other center gold 11º on the second pearl component. Pick up an 11º gold, a cube, and an 11º gold. Sew through the matching center bead on the first pearl

Since the thread in the final round of beads needs to be quite snug, the beading adage "Pull the thread, not the needle" is especially appropriate to keep from fraying and breaking the thread.

component so the two sets of beads form links between two pearl components **(figure 2)**. Reinforce the thread path.

14 Repeat steps 11–13 to attach each pearl component.

15 Sew a split ring to each end of the bracelet using the center 11º gold. This is the bottom bead of the right-angle weave strip in steps 2 and 3, and it is just below the beads from steps 12 and 13.

16 Use jump rings to attach half of the clasp to a split ring at each end.

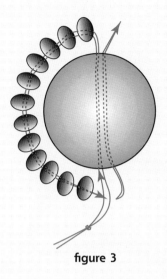

figure 3

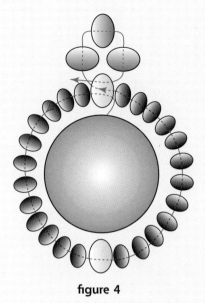

figure 4

If the 15ºs around the outside of the pearl disk won't stay in place, use a small dab of G-S Hypo Cement to secure them. You can also use cement to seal the cut in the jump ring.

EARRINGS

1 For each earring: Follow steps 1–9 of the bracelet.

2 Work the needle to a corner of the pearl component, and exit an 11º red. Stitch an 11º gold between the two 11º reds on the corner. Reinforce. Attach a 4–5mm jump ring to an earring post. Pick up four 11º golds and the 4–5mm jump ring, and sew back through the 11º gold just picked up, making a small loop. Reinforce, and end the thread.

3 On a doubled and knotted thread, pick up a round pearl disk. Pick up approximately 12 15ºs. Slide the beads down to the knot, and pass the needle between the threads. Sew up through the disk again **(figure 3)**. Pull the 15ºs tight against the disk.

4 Pick up approximately 12 15ºs, and sew up through the disk again, positioning the 15ºs on the opposite side of the disk to form a ring of 15ºs around the disk.

5 Pick up an 11º gold, and sew through the 15ºs on one side of the pearl. Pick up an 11º gold, and sew through the 15ºs on the other side of the disk.

6 Sew through the first 11º gold picked up, and pick up three 11º reds. Sew back

through the 11º gold again to make a small loop like a picot **(figure 4)**. Repeat the thread path to reinforce.

7 Sew through the 15º on one side of the disk and the other 11º gold picked up in step 5. Sew one 11º gold to it, as in ladder stitch, to make a short stem.

8 Sew the 11º gold just picked up to an 11º red on the corner of the pearl component opposite the loop to attach the disk. Reinforce the thread path, and end the thread.

My pearls were not very thick. The double-sided tape added some thickness, so they fit the beadwork better. Depending on your pearls, you may not need the extra thickness, but the double-sided tape also holds the pearl in place as you stitch.

LAVISH LEAF
Lariat and Earrings

If you are a fool for fringe, then this is the necklace for you! Stitch easy spiral rope and leaf fringe trimmed with cobalt drop beads.

MATERIALS

Lariat, 36 in. (.9m)

50 grams 11º silver-lined dark gold seed beads

10 grams 11º opaque cobalt blue seed beads

18 grams 4mm silver-lined cobalt magatama drops

Earrings, 1¾ in. (4.4cm) long

2 grams 11º silver-lined dark gold seed beads

3 grams 4mm silver-lined cobalt magatama drops

Pair of gold earring findings

2 4mm gold jump rings

2 pairs of chainnose pliers

Both

Beading thread

Needle

Scissors

STITCHES

Spiral rope, p. 15

Fringe, p. 15

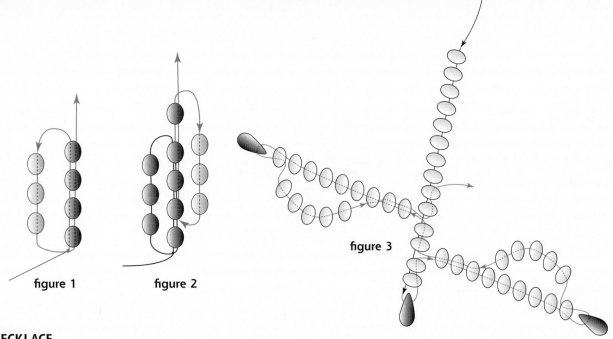

figure 1

figure 2

figure 3

NECKLACE

Begin Spiral Rope

1 On a comfortable length of thread, begin making a spiral rope: Pick up four 11º cobalt blue seed beads and three 11º silver-lined dark gold seed beads, and tie the beads into a circle, pushing the golds to the left side. Sew through the four cobalts again **(figure 1)**.

2 Pick up a cobalt and three golds. Sew through the last three cobalts plus the one just picked up **(figure 2)**. Push the golds to the left.

3 Repeat step 2 until the spiral rope is approximately 30 in. (76cm) long.

Make the Fringe

4 Exiting from the cobalts at the center of the spiral rope, pick up 5 in. (13cm) of golds.

5 Pick up a cobalt magatama drop. Sew back through the last two golds picked up in step 4.

6 Pick up nine golds and a drop, and sew back through the last gold. Pick up five golds, skip five golds on the fringe stem, and sew through the remaining

three golds to return to the main stem. Sew through two beads on the main stem **(figure 3)**.

7 Repeat step 6 until you reach the spiral rope. At the spiral rope, sew up through the cobalts, making a couple of half-hitch knots, before returning to the end of the spiral rope to start the next fringe.

8 Anchor a new fringe in the spiral rope, and pick up golds for 4 in. (10cm).

9 Repeat steps 5–7.

> Make a few half-hitch knots as you are adding the leaf fringe in case the thread in one breaks.

10 Anchor a new fringe in the spiral rope, and pick up golds for 2½ in. (6.4cm).

11 Repeat steps 5–7. End the thread in the spiral rope instead of returning to the end of the spiral rope.

12 Attach a thread at the other end of the spiral rope, and repeat steps 4–9 to create one fringe 5-in. long and one fringe 4-in. long.

Make the Adjustment Ring

13 Repeat steps 1 and 2 to make a spiral rope 1½-in. (3.8cm) long. It should wrap snugly around the two necklace strands, but move easily to adjust the fall of the fringes.

14 Adjust the length of the spiral rope from step 13 if necessary. Then sew the ends together firmly to make a ring around the necklace just above the fringe.

15 From the point where the ring joins, follow steps 4–9, picking up 2½ and then 1½ in. of golds in step 4.

EARRINGS

1 For both earrings: On a comfortable length of thread, pick up five golds. Make a circle by sewing through all the beads three times.

2 Exiting a gold, string 1 in. (2.5cm) of golds, pick up a drop, and sew back through two golds. Follow the necklace steps 6 and 7 to make leaf fringe. End the threads in the bead circle.

3 Attach the beadwork to the earring finding with a jump ring.

GOLDEN TWIST
Necklace and Bracelet

This dramatic necklace is based on a Dutch spiral stitch. Make the twist first, and then create the rest of the necklace. The changing bugle bead size creates the exciting twist with tight turns between the beads.

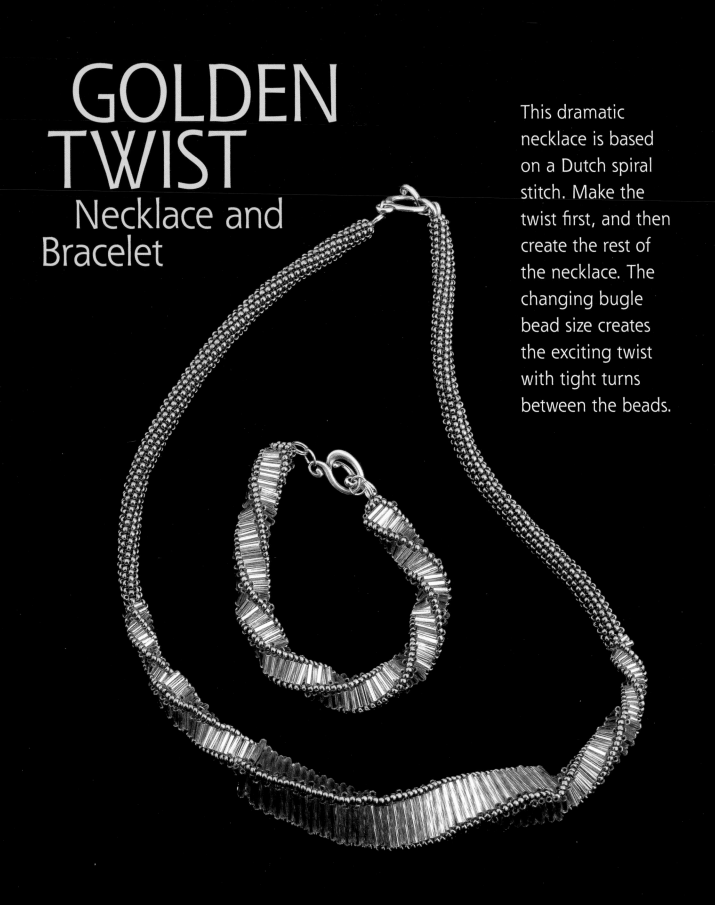

MATERIALS

Necklace, 22 in. (56cm) including clasp

13 grams size 5 silver-lined gold twisted bugle beads (large)

5 grams size 3 silver-lined gold bugle beads (medium)

2 grams size 1 silver-lined gold bugle beads (small)

14 grams 11º smoky gold bronze seed beads

Bracelet, 8 in. (20cm), including clasp

15 grams medium (#3) silver-lined gold bugle beads

5 grams 11º smoky gold bronze seed beads

Both

Fireline

4 5mm gold split rings

4 5mm gold jump rings

Toggle clasp

Needles

Scissors

2 pairs of chainnose pliers

STITCHES

Dutch spiral, p. 17

Odd-count tubular peyote, p. 90

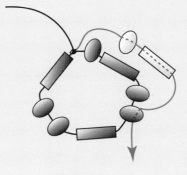

figure 1

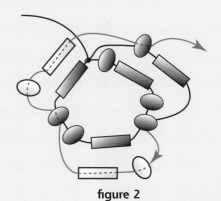

figure 2

NECKLACE
Begin Dutch Spiral

1 On a comfortable length of thread, pick up an 11º seed bead, a small bugle bead, two 11ºs, a small bugle, two 11ºs and a small bugle. Tie the beads into a cicle with a firm knot, leaving a 10-in. (25cm) tail.

> Make frequent half-hitch knots as you stitch to hold tension and keep the piece from unraveling if the thread breaks.

2 For the next round, pick up an 11º and a small bugle. Skip the next 11º, small bugle, and 11º in the original ring, and sew through the next 11º **(figure 1)**. Keep the tension snug.

3 Pick up an 11º and a small bugle. Skip the next small bugle and 11º, and sew through the second 11º **(figure 2)**. Force the new beads to the top of the rope with your fingers.

4 Repeat step 3, stepping up through the first 11º picked up in step 2. Stack the bugles on top of each other; shape the twisted three-sided rope as you go.

> Before starting the twist, count out the beads needed for each section, discarding any damaged bugles. The completed rows are difficult to count as you work the twist.

5 Repeat step 4, 14 times.

6 Repeat step 4, transitioning to medium bugle beads by substituting one in each round, for three rounds.

7 Repeat step 4, using all medium bugles, for 20 rounds.

8 Repeat step 4, transitioning to large bugle beads by substituting one in each round, for three rounds.

9 Repeat step 4, using all large bugles, for 55 rounds.

10 Repeat step 4, transitioning to medium bugles by substituting one in each round, for three rounds.

11 Repeat step 4, using all medium bugles, for 20 rounds.

12 Repeat step 4, transitioning to small bugles by substituting one in each round, for three rounds.

13 Repeat step 4, using all small bugles, for 16 rounds.

14 Sew through each 11º in the spine to close up any gaps and to reinforce the twist.

15 Use the remaining thread on the end of the twist or attach a new thread. Pick up two 11ºs between each 11º on the end of the twist to create a circle of nine 11ºs.

16 Work odd-count tubular peyote for 6 in. (15cm). Sew through the top four beads and pull snug. Sew on a split ring. End the thread in the tube.

17 Repeat steps 15 and 16 at the other end of the twist.

18 Attach a clasp half to each end of the necklace with a jump ring.

It may be helpful to use a small dowel or toothpick to start and end the twist and to start the odd-count tubular peyote sections.

Add thread by either knotting a new thread onto the old with a square or surgeon's knot, leaving long tails to work in later, or by using two needles. With the two-needle method, secure the working thread with a half-hitch knot. Drop the old needle and thread. Prepare a new needle and thread. Starting a few beads below the old thread, follow the thread path through the beads, making a few half-hitch knots as you go. Exit the same bead as the old thread. Keeping the two sets of threads carefully away from each other, secure the old thread in the beadwork with half-hitch knots, and trim.

BRACELET

1 Follow the instructions for the twist portion of the necklace, using only medium bugle beads. Make the bracelet about 1 in. (2.5cm) longer than you want the finished bracelet (as you reinforce the spines, it shortens the bracelet). Do not use tight tension, or your bracelet will be stiff.

2 Exiting an 11º at the end of the bracelet, pick up three 11ºs and sew through the top 11º of the next spine. Repeat around the tube, picking up nine 11ºs, for a total of 12.

3 Work tubular peyote, decreasing two stitches each round, to make a blunt end. To decrease: Instead of picking up a new 11º to make the next stitch, leave the space empty and pass through the next 11º. When there are two 11ºs left, use them to sew on a split ring.

4 Repeat steps 2 and 3 on the other end of the bracelet.

5 Attach a clasp half to each end of the necklace with a jump ring.

OPPOSITES ATTRACT
Bracelet

This pair of bracelets plays with perception. Both bracelets use exactly the same graphic patterns, but in opposite colors. The difference in the look of each bead is remarkable.

MATERIALS

2 bracelets, 8 in. (20cm) each including clasp

7 8mm round gold beads

7 8mm round black beads

2 6mm round gold beads

2 6mm round black beads

5 grams 8º black beads

6 grams gold 11º cylinder bead

6 grams black 11º cylinder beads

4 gold crimp beads

2 gold clasps

Beading thread

24 in. (61cm) beading wire, cut in half

Needle

Scissors

Crimping pliers

Wire cutters

STITCHES

Flat odd-count peyote stitch, p. 89

Zipping up, p. 90

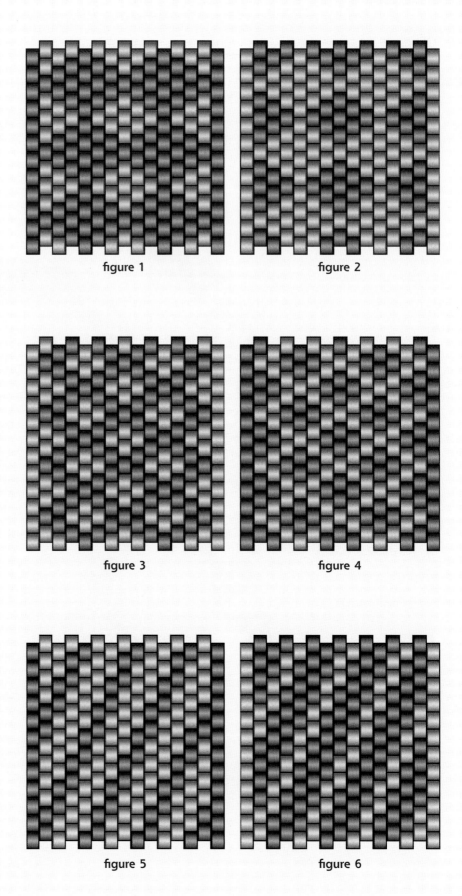

figure 1

figure 2

figure 3

figure 4

figure 5

figure 6

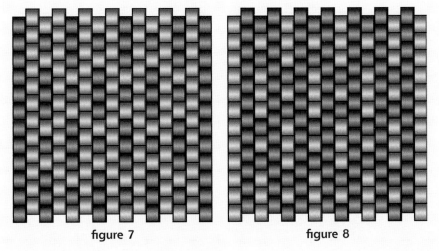

figure 7

figure 8

BRACELET

1 On a comfortable length of thread, work odd-count peyote stitch using black and gold cylinder beads following the illustration **(figure 1)**. Zip up the ends to make a bead tube. Repeat with the remaining charts **(figures 2–12)**. These charts are arranged to be worked left to right, bottom up.

2 Separate the beads and bead tubes into materials for two bracelets: Arrange the bead tubes in two rows, with each bead's opposite next to it. For the bead tubes with black borders on the ends, use 8mm and 6mm gold round beads as spacers. For those with gold borders, use 8mm and 6mm black round beads as spacers.

3 For each bracelet: String a crimp bead and half of the clasp on the beading wire. Pass the beading wire back through the crimp bead. Crimp, and trim the excess wire.

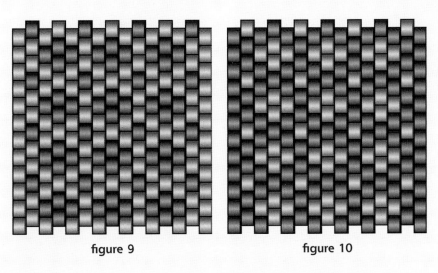

figure 9

figure 10

4 String a 6mm, an 8mm, and a bead tube. Fill the bead tubes with seven 8º black filler beads. Continue alternating 8mms and bead tubes until all six bead tubes are strung. Finish by stringing an 8mm, a 6mm, a crimp bead, and the other half of the clasp.

5 Pass the beading wire back through the crimp. Pull snug. Crimp, and trim the excess wire.

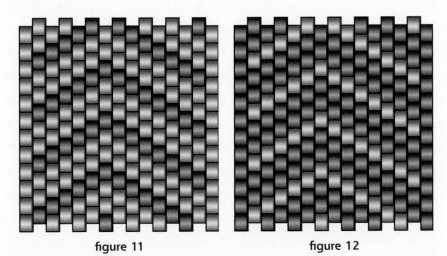

figure 11

figure 12

ST. PETERSBURG
Choker and Earrings

This easy, elegant set features the timeless combination of turquoise and coral with gold.

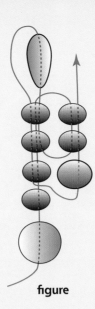

figure

MATERIALS

Choker, 17 in. (43cm) including clasp

68 6x4mm turquoise drop (fringe) beads (about 10 grams)

68 6º dark coral red seed beads (about 7 grams)

8 grams 8º gold seed beads

Box clasp

Earrings, 1½ in. (3.8cm)

6 6x4mm turquoise drop (fringe) beads

2 dark coral red 6º seed beads

1 gram 11º gold seed beads

Pair 8mm half-dome post earring findings with loop

2 6mm jump rings

Both

Beading thread

Needle

Scissors

2 pairs of chainnose pliers

STITCH

St. Petersburg chain stitch, p. 94

CHOKER

1 On a comfortable length of thread, work St. Petersburg chain stitch, starting with 8º gold seed beads and using 6x4mm turquoise drop beads in step 3 and 6º dark coral red seed beads in step 4 on p. 94 **(figure)**. Continue for 16½ in. (41.9cm).

2 Stitch a clasp half to each end of the necklace.

You may want to put a tiny drop of glue on the split in the jump ring to prevent either the fringe threads or the earring loop from slipping through it.

EARRINGS

1 For each earring: Tie 2 ft. (61cm) of thread onto a 6mm jump ring, positioning the knot opposite the split in the jump ring.

2 Pick up a 6º, 12 11ºs, and a drop. Skipping the drop, sew back through the 11ºs and 6º, loop around the jump ring, and sew back through the 6º to make a fringe.

3 Pick up 10 11ºs and a drop. Skipping the drop, sew back through the 11ºs and 6º, loop around the jump ring, and sew back through the 6º.

4 Pick up eight 11ºs and a drop. Skipping the drop, sew back through the 11ºs and 6º, loop around the jump ring, and sew back through the 6º.

5 End the thread in one of the fringes with a couple of half-hitch knots.

6 Attach the jump ring to the earring finding.

OLD COINS
Necklace

Coins have always been used in jewelry. Here is one featuring pennies, but you could use any comparably sized disk—perhaps even ancient Roman coins!

MATERIALS

Necklace, 34 in. (86cm)

4 old copper US pennies or similar-sized coins

25 grams 8º gold seed beads

5 grams 11º dark steel seed beads

2 grams 11º silver-lined crystal seed beads

3 grams 11º gold seed beads

2 grams 15º crystal silver luster seed beads

2 grams 15º gold seed beads

Beading thread

Needles

Scissors

STITCHES

Even-count tubular peyote stitch, p. 90

Square stitch, p. 91

Circular right-angle weave, p. 93

> Use the instructions in the "Stitch Basics" section for circular right-angle weave.

NECKLACE
Make Bezeled Coins

1 On a comfortable length of thread, pick up six 11º dark steel seed beads. Tie the 11ºs into a circle, and sew through the first 11º picked up.

2 Work a right-angle weave increase stitch with 11º dark steels on each 11º picked up in step 1. The finished round will have 12 11ºs on the outer edge. Step up through the first 11º picked up to start the next round.

3 Work a right-angle weave stitch with 11º dark steels. Increase on every other 11º picked up in step 2. The finished round will have 18 11ºs. Step up to start the next round.

4 Work a right-angle weave stitch with 11º dark steels. Increase on every third 11º picked up in step 3. The finished round will have 24 11ºs. Step up to start the next round.

5 Work a right-angle weave stitch on every 11º dark steel picked up in step 4 using 15º crystal silver luster seed beads. The finished row will have 24 15ºs. Step up to start the next round.

6 Work a right-angle weave stitch on every 15º picked up in step 5, using 15º crystal silver lusters, except pick up a 15º gold seed bead so it is the top bead in the right-angle weave stitch each time. The finished round will have 24 beads.

7 Center a coin in the beadwork.

8 Sew a 15º gold between each 15º gold picked up in step 6. Pull snug.

9 Work around the last round again to reinforce the thread path, and pull snug. End the thread.

10 Attach a new thread, and exit an 11º dark steel in the last row. Sew an 11º gold seed bead between each 11º dark steel on this row, as you would for peyote stitch. The 11º dark steels are the top beads of the right-angle weave stitches in step 4.

11 Sew an 11º gold between each 11º gold picked up in step 10.

12 Sew an 11º silver-lined crystal seed bead between each 11º gold picked up in step 11. Work around this round again to reinforce the thread path, and end the threads.

13 Repeat steps 1–12 three times for a total of four encased coins.

Make Necklace Connectors

14 On a comfortable length of thread, using 8º gold seed beads, work a square stitch strip three beads wide for 14 in. (36cm) (about 120 rows).

15 Repeat step 14, but make a strip 7 in. (18cm) long (about 60 rows).

16 Repeat step 14, but make two strips 3½ in. (8.9cm) long (about 30 rows).

17 Attach an encased coin to each end of the 3½-in. strips: Align the square stitches next to a crystal–gold–crystal segment at the top (and bottom) of the coin. Square stitch through the beads on the coin and the beads on the square stitch strip.

18 Connect the unit created in step 17 to the 7-in. strip from step 15, to form the front of the necklace.

19 Connect the tops of the remaining two coins with the 14-in. strip from step 14.

TRIPLE ST. PETERSBURG
Bracelet

St. Petersburg chain stitch makes a wonderfully flexible and intricate-looking bracelet. So let's triple it for even more impact and style!

MATERIALS

Bracelet, 8 in. (20cm) including clasp

5 grams 8º seed beads, purple or blue iris

10 grams 11º seed beads, gold or bronze

Beading thread

Needle

Scissors

STITCHES

Even-count flat peyote stitch, p. 89

Ladder stitch, p. 90

St. Petersburg chain stitch, p. 94

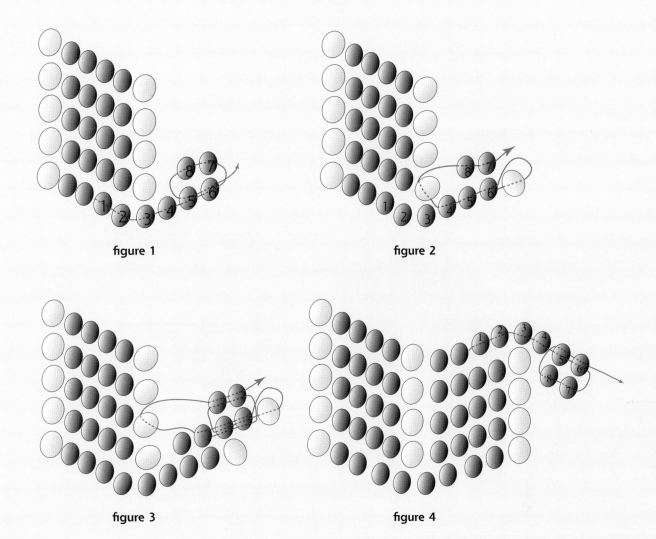

figure 1

figure 2

figure 3

figure 4

BRACELET

Make the Chain

1 On a comfortable length of thread, work St. Petersburg chain stitch, starting with 11º gold or bronze seed beads and using 8º purple or blue iris seed beads for the accent beads picked up in steps 3 and 4 on p. 94. Continue for 7½ in. (18cm).

2 To start the second row, pick up eight 11ºs, and sew through the fifth and sixth 11ºs again. You will be working back toward the starting row. Be sure the beads are positioned so the first chain and the new row make the V shape **(figure 1)**.

3 Pick up an 8º, and sew back through three 11ºs. Sew through an 8º on the chain made in step 1 and two 11ºs picked up in step 2 as shown **(figure 2)**.

4 Pick up four 11ºs, and sew through the first two 11ºs again, pushing them up. Pick up an 8º, and sew back through three 11ºs as in step 3. Sew through the next 8º on the chain from step 1 and the two 11ºs just picked up **(figure 3)**.

5 Repeat step 4 for the length of the bracelet.

6 To start the third row, pick up eight 11ºs and sew through the fifth and sixth beads again, pushing the beads down. Position the beadwork so the third row creates a V shape **(figure 4)**.

7 Repeat step 3, using an 8º from row 2 and the last two 11ºs picked up.

8 Work step 4 for the length of the bracelet, pushing the beads down each time.

9 To make the ending stitch the same as the others in the row, pick up two 11ºs and an 8º. Skipping the 8º, sew back through the 11º into the beadwork. Repeat the thread paths in the stitches at the end of the bracelet to provide additional stability, if needed, and end the threads.

10 Remove the stop bead. Pick up an 8º. Stitch back into the beadwork to complete the stitch the same as the others in the row. Repeat the thread paths in the stitches at the end of the bracelet to provide additional stability, if needed, and end the thread.

Add the Toggle Clasp

11 On a new thread, pick up 10 11ºs and work flat peyote stitch for eight rows. Zip the ends together to make a tube. Exiting one end of the tube, pick up an 8º and an 11º. Skipping the last 11º, sew through the 8º, and continue through the tube to the other side. Pick up an 8º and an 11º. Skipping the last 11º, sew back through the 8º and reinforce the thread path between the two beads just added to the ends of the bead tube.

12 Exiting the center of the bead tube, work a ladder stitch two beads wide for five stitches to make the toggle stem.

13 Attach the stem of the toggle to one end of the bracelet. End the thread in the bracelet **(photo a)**.

14 At the other end of the bracelet, attach a thread and work three ladder stitches two-beads wide using 11ºs. Exiting one side of the last ladder stitch, pick up 24 11ºs. Sew through the last ladder stitch to make a loop. Reinforce the thread path several times, and end the threads **(photo b)**.

GOLD LACE
Cuff

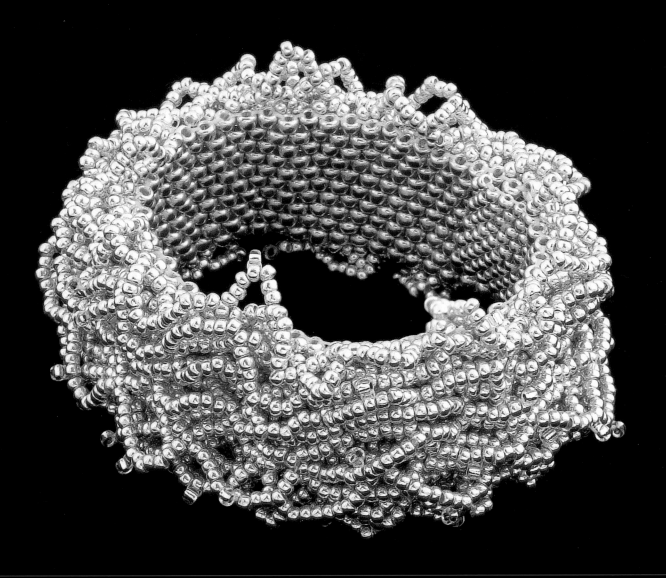

A lavish amount of netting creates an old-fashioned lacy cuff with a nearly invisible clasp opening. The gold lace is dotted with silver-lined crystal beads for a bit of extra flash.

MATERIALS

Cuff, 6½ in. (16.5cm)

15 grams 8º gold
seed beads

40 grams 11º gold
seed beads

3 or more grams 11º
silver-lined crystal
seed beads

Size 4/0 snap

Beading thread

Needle

Scissors

STITCHES

Netting, p. 30

Even-count flat peyote
stitch, p. 89

BRACELET
Make the
Peyote Base

1 On a comfortable
length of thread,
pick up 10 8º gold
seed beads. Work
even-count flat
peyote stitch for
6½ in. (16.5cm).

2 Using 11º gold seed
beads, work flat peyote stitch
for 12 rows to make a tab for the
snap clasp. End the threads.

Add Netting Rows

3 Attach a new thread and exit the
first 8º in an outside bracelet row. Pick
up three 11º golds. Skip an 8º, and sew
through the next 8º, from the inside to
the outside. The three 11º golds will lie
diagonally on the 8º base. Continue
to the end of the row, adding three
11º golds between every other 8º as
shown. This completes the first row of
netting on an outside column (row)
of the peyote base **(figure 1; black
arrows show the first three base
peyote rows)**.

Adjust the
length of the
bracelet by adding
more rows of peyote
in 8ºs to the
base.

4 Pick up enough 11º golds
to make a partial loop (I
used two), and sew through
the middle 11º gold of the
first loop of netting on the
previous row. Pick up five 11º
golds. Sew through the middle
11º gold of the next netting loop.
Continue across the row **(figure 2)**.

As you work the netting
on the peyote base, not all
rows will end with a complete loop.
Adjust the last netting loop to create
a loop comparable to the other loops in
the row. You'll need to do this at each
end to create end loops that look full
enough. I work them as I go, but you
can always come back later and
fill in to even things up.

5 Pick up as many 11º golds as needed
for a partial loop (I used three), and
sew through the middle 11º gold of
the first five-bead loop of netting on
the previous row. Add crystal seed
beads to the middle bead of the loop
by picking up four 11º golds and one
11º crystal seed bead. Sew through the
last gold 11º again, and pull the 11º
crystal snugly on top of the gold bead.
Pick up three 11ºs, and sew through
the middle bead of the next netting
loop. Continue across the row. You can
add as many or as few 11º crystals as
you desire. The diagram shows one on
every other loop **(figure 3)**.

6 Make a partial loop to finish this row.
End the thread.

7 Continue adding rows of netting to
the peyote base.

Peyote Base Row 1
Netting Row 1: three size 11ºs, starting in the first 8º (steps 3–6 above) base bead, then every other bead
Netting Row 2: five size 11ºs
Netting Row 3: seven size 11º golds plus 11º crystals
Peyote Base Row 2
Netting Row 1: five 11º golds, starting in the first 8º base bead, then every third bead
Netting Row 2: seven 11º golds
Netting Row 3: nine 11º golds plus 11º crystals
Peyote Base Row 3: Repeat Peyote Base Row 2
Peyote Base Row 4
Netting Row 1: seven 11º golds, starting in the first 8º base bead, then every fourth bead
Netting Row 2: nine beads
Netting Row 3: 11º golds plus 11º crystals
Peyote Base Row 5
Netting Row 1: nine beads, starting in the first 8º base bead, then every fourth bead
Netting Row 2: 11º golds
Netting Row 3: 11º golds plus 11º crystals
Peyote Base Row 6: Repeat Peyote Base Row 5
Peyote Base Row 7: Repeat Peyote Base Row 4
Peyote Base Row 8: Repeat Peyote Base Row 3
Peyote Base Row 9: Repeat Peyote Base Row 2
Peyote Base Row 10: Repeat Peyote Base Row 1

Finish the Bracelet

8 Sew a snap on the top of the 11º peyote tab created in step 2. Sew the other half of the snap to the underside of the peyote base.

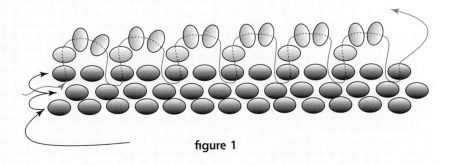

figure 1

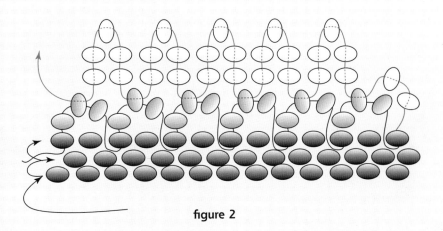

figure 2

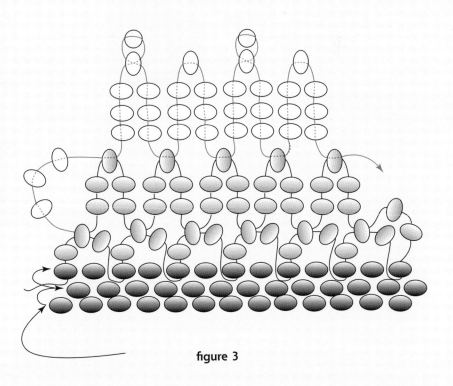

figure 3

TRIANGLE MEETS CUBE
Bracelet

MATERIALS

Bracelet, 9 in. (23cm) including clasp

- 6 grams 3mm gold cube beads
- 6 grams 8º bronze iris triangles
- 4 grams 11º smoky gold bronze seed beads
- 2 6mm gold split rings
- 5mm gold jump ring
- Lobster claw clasp
- Beading thread or Fireline
- Needle
- Scissors
- 2 pairs of chainnose pliers

STITCHES

- Square stitch, p. 91
- Brick stitch, p. 91

Pair two easy stitches to make a handsome gold-and-bronze bracelet.

figure 1

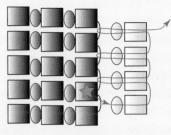

figure 2

BRACELET

Make Rectangles

1 On a comfortable length of beading thread or Fireline, pick up a 3mm gold cube bead, an 11º smoky gold bronze seed bead, a cube, an 11º, and a cube for a total of five beads.

2 Pick up a cube, and work in square stitch to attach it to the cube on the previous row.

3 Pick up an 11º and a cube. Work in square stitch to attach the cube to the cube on the previous row, letting the 11º "float" between the cubes.

4 Repeat step 3.

5 Repeat steps 2–4 three times for a total of five rows. End the thread.

6 Repeat steps 1–5 five times for a total of six gold cube rectangles.

Stitch Triangle Connectors

7 Attach a thread to one of the gold cube rectangles, exiting an edge cube.

8 Pick up an 11º and an 8º bronze iris triangle. Repeat three times, and pick up an 11º.

9 Sew through an edge cube on another rectangle. Exit the adjacent cube bead, going back toward the starting rectangle **(figure 1)**.

10 Repeat steps 8 and 9 for the other rows of cubes in the rectangle.

11 When all the cube rows in the two rectangles have triangles and 11ºs strung between them, work the needle to the opposite side of a rectangle.

12 Repeat steps 8–11 four times to connect all the gold rectangles with triangle and 11º connectors.

Shorten the bracelet by leaving out one of the rectangle sections (1¼ in./3.2cm).

Finish with Decreasing Cubes

13 Attach a thread to a rectangle on one end of the bracelet, and exit an edge cube in the second row. Pick up an 11º, two cubes, and an 11º. Work brick stitch by passing under the thread between the second and third cubes and back up through the second 11º and cube picked up in this step.

14 Work two more two-drop (11º and cube) brick stitches, picking up a cube bead and an 11º each time, for a total of four cubes on this row **(figure 2)**.

15 Stepping one cube inward, work two-drop 11º and cube brick stitches for the next row (three cubes).

16 Stepping one cube inward, work two-drop 11º and cube brick stitches for the next row (two cubes).

17 Make a half-hitch knot in the center of the thread bridge between the two cube beads in the last row (step 16). Pick up an 11º, a cube, and an 11º, skip the last 11º, and sew back through the cube and 11º. Secure the thread in the body of the bracelet. Sew back through the 11º and cube, exiting the final 11º. Sew on a split ring, and end the thread.

18 At the other end of the bracelet, repeat steps 13–17.

19 Use a 5mm jump ring to attach the clasp to one end of the bracelet.

SUMMER LACE
Necklace and Earrings

MATERIALS

Necklace, 4 ft. (1.23m)

6mm round pearl

4mm round pearl

4 grams 6 6º pearl seed beads

12 grams 11º rose gold seed beads

Earrings, approximately ⁷⁄₈ in. (2.2cm)

2 6mm round pearl beads

2 4mm round pearl beads

1 gram 11º rose gold seed beads

Pair rose gold earring findings

Both

Beading thread

Needle

Scissors

STITCHES

Ladder stitch, p. 90

Right-angle weave, p. 92

Create a lacy necklace in romantic rose gold with pearls and a tiny pendant accent.

NECKLACE

Make the Chain

1 Begin right-angle weave: On a comfortable length of thread, pick up four 11º rose gold seed beads. Tie the 11ºs into a circle, and sew through the next two 11ºs.

2 Pick up three 11ºs. Sew through the 11º exited at the start of this step to form a circle. Sew through the next two 11ºs, exiting the middle 11º.

3 Repeat step 2.

4 Sew an 11º to the top of the last 11º exited.

5 Pick up 11 11ºs, and sew back through the 11º first exited to form a circle.

6 Pick up a 6º pearl seed bead. Sew through the 11º directly across on the circle.

7 Pick up an 11º, and sew it to the 11º just exited **(figure 1)**.

8 Pick up three 11ºs. Sew through the 11º picked up in step 7 to form a circle. Continue through the 11ºs, exiting the middle 11º.

9 Repeat steps 2–8 for 4 ft. (1.23m). Remember that right-angle weave changes direction with each stitch.

10 Sew the beginning and ending 11ºs together, picking up 11ºs if necessary to keep the pattern intact. End the thread.

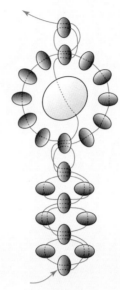

figure 1

Make the Pendant

11 On a doubled and knotted thread, pick up a 6mm round pearl and eight 11ºs. Slide the beads down to the knot, and pass the needle between the threads. Pull the 11ºs tight against the pearl. Sew through the pearl again **(figure 2)**.

12 Pick up eight 11ºs, and sew through the pearl again, positioning the 11ºs on the opposite side of the pearl to form a ring of 11ºs around the pearl.

13 Reinforce the thread path, and sew through the 11ºs again, exiting the last 11º at the bottom of the pearl.

14 Pick up an 11º, a 4mm round pearl, and an 11º. Skipping the 11º, sew through the 4mm pearl, 11º just picked up, and 6mm pearl.

15 Sew through an 11º directly next to one side of the pearl bead hole. Pick up two 11ºs, and sew back through the adjacent 11º and the first 11º exited **(figure 3)**.

figure 2

figure 3

16 Using these two beads as a base, work ladder stitch for nine rows.

17 Wrap the ladder stitch band around the necklace between two pearl segments. Sew the end of the ladder band to the ladder stitch directly above the pearl. Reinforce and end the thread.

EARRINGS

1 For each earring: Repeat steps 11–15 of the necklace instructions.

2 Pick up five 11ºs, and sew back through the two 11ºs picked up in step 15, forming a loop. Reinforce the thread path.

3 Open an earring finding and attach the loop.

BUGLE BOY BANDS
Bracelet

Revel in this handsome bracelet made with a flexible stitch. The banded beads are fun to slide, twirl, and fidget with.

MATERIALS

Bracelet, 8¾ in. (22.2cm) including clasp

15 size 3 silver-lined silver bugle beads

30 size 3 silver-lined gold bugle beads

10 grams 8º bronze metallic seed beads

1 gram 11º silver seed beads

1 gram 11º gold seed beads

½ gram 15º silver seed beads

½ gram 15º gold seed beads

2 5mm gold split rings

5mm gold jump ring

Lobster claw clasp

Beading thread or Fireline

Needle

Scissors

2 pairs of chainnose pliers

STITCHES

Ladder stitch, p. 90

Tubular right-angle weave, p. 92

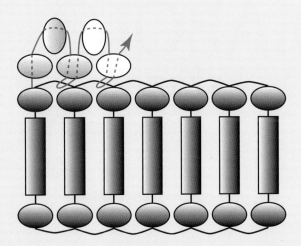

figure

NECKLACE

Make the Bracelet Rope

1 On a comfortable length of thread, pick up four 8º bronze seed beads, leaving an 8-in. (20cm) tail. Tie the 8ºs into a circle.

2 Work two more right-angle weave stitches. Join the ends to make a ring of four stitches.

3 Work tubular right-angle weave until the rope is 8 in. (20cm) long.

4 Sew through all the 8ºs on the end of the rope. Pull snug. Sew a split ring to the end of the rope. End the thread.

5 Using the tail thread at the other end of the bracelet, repeat step 4.

Make Bands

6 Pick up an 11º gold seed bead, a size 3 silver-lined silver bugle bead, two 11º golds, a silver bugle, and an 11º gold. Work ladder stitch for a total of 15 bugle beads (each 11º–bugle–11º set is one rung of the ladder). Join the ends to form a bugle band.

7 Exiting an 11º on the edge of the band, pick up three 15º gold seed beads. Sew under the first loop of thread immediately to the right of the bead exited and back up through the last 15º gold. This forms a picot.

8 Pick up two 15º golds. Sew under the next loop of thread to the right and back up through the second 15º gold, forming another picot **(figure)**.

9 Repeat step 8 around the edge of the band, joining the first and last picots with a single 15º gold.

10 Work the needle to the other side of the bugle band, and repeat steps 7–9. End the thread.

11 Repeat steps 6–10 using size 3 silver-lined gold bugle beads and 11º silver seed beads. Make two gold bugle bands.

12 Slide the bands on the bracelet.

13 Use a jump ring to attach the clasp to one split ring.

DIABOLO
Necklace

Dutch spiral and its many variations have been popular since Gineke Root's *Innovative Beaded Jewelry Techniques* was published in 1994, translated from the original Dutch. The Diabolo variation is worked as an integral part of this necklace.

MATERIALS

Necklace, 19½ in. (49.5cm) including clasp

2 grams 5mm bronze bugle beads

4 grams 6º metallic beads

8 grams 8º metallic seed beads

20 grams 11º bronze seed beads

Beading thread

Fireline (optional for Dutch spiral portion)

Needle

Scissors

STITCHES

Modified Dutch spiral, p. 39

Even-count flat peyote stitch, p. 89

Tubular herringbone, p. 91

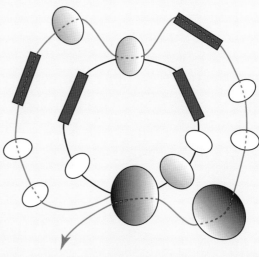

figure 1

You may want to change to Fireline or use doubled thread for the spiral portion of the necklace.

If you want to make the necklace longer or shorter, adjust the number of herringbone rows on each end of the necklace.

NECKLACE

Begin the Rope

1 On a comfortable length of thread, pick up six 11º bronze seed beads, leaving an 8-in. (20cm) tail. Tie the 11ºs into a circle.

2 Work tubular herringbone stitch with 11ºs for 36 rows.

3 Work tubular herringbone stitch with 8º metallic seed beads for one row.

4 Work tubular herringbone stitch with 11ºs for 20 rows.

5 Work tubular herringbone stitch with 8ºs for two rows.

6 Work tubular herringbone stitch with 11ºs for 19 rows.

7 Work tubular herringbone stitch with 8ºs for three rows.

8 Work tubular herringbone stitch with 11ºs for 17 rows.

9 Work tubular herringbone stitch with 8ºs for four rows.

Begin the Modified Dutch (Diabolo) Spiral

10 Pick up a 6º metallic seed bead, an 11º, and a bronze bugle bead. Sew down through the fourth 8º in the previous row. Pick up a bugle and an 11º, and sew through the sixth (last) 8º and the 6º in the beginning of this row.

11 Pick up two 11ºs, a bugle, and an 8º, and sew through the 8º in the previous row. Pick up a bugle, two 11ºs, and a 6º. Sew through the 6º in the original row again **(figure 1)**.

12 Pick up three 11ºs, a bugle, and an 8º, and sew through the 8º in the previous row. Pick up a bugle, three 11ºs, and a 6º. Sew through the 6º in the previous row.

13 Repeat step 12, using four 11ºs each time instead of three.

14 Repeat step 12, using five 11ºs each time instead of three.

15 Repeat step 12, using six 11ºs each time instead of three.

16 Repeat step 12, using seven 11ºs each time instead of three.

17 Repeat step 16 for 22 rows.

18 Repeat steps 11–15 in reverse order to taper the end of the Diabolo spiral.

19 Pick up an 11º, a bugle, and an 8º, and sew through the 8º in the previous row. Pick up a bugle, an 11º, and a 6º. Sew through the 6º in the previous row.

20 Sew through all the 8ºs in the Diabolo spiral, and return through all of the 6ºs to tighten and shape the spiral.

21 Exit the last 6º, pick up two 8ºs, and sew through the 8º in the previous row. Pick up two 8ºs, and sew through the 6º again. This uses the 6º as the sixth bead of the starting herringbone row. Locate the six beads you will use to start the herringbone stitch. This is row 1 of the herringbone rope on this side of the necklace.

22 Pick up two 8ºs, sew through the next two 8ºs, pick up two 8ºs, and sew through the next two 8ºs. For the last stitch on this row, pick up two 8ºs, and sew through the 8º and the 6º. Step up through the beads in the first stitch.

23 Work tubular herringbone stitch using 8ºs for two rows. This is a total of four rows after the Diabolo spiral.

24 Work tubular herringbone stitch using 11ºs for 17 rows.

25 Work tubular herringbone stitch using 8ºs for three rows.

26 Work tubular herringbone stitch using 11ºs for 19 rows.

27 Work tubular herringbone stitch using 8ºs for two rows.

28 Work tubular herringbone stitch using 11ºs for 20 rows.

29 Work tubular herringbone stitch using 8ºs for one row.

30 Work tubular herringbone stitch using 11ºs for 37 rows.

31 Taper the end of the rope by picking up an 11º, skipping an 11º, and sewing through the next 11º. Repeat twice. Sew through the three remaining 11ºs and pull snug. End the thread in the beadwork. Repeat this step at the other end of the necklace with the tail thread.

Add the Clasp

32 Make the toggle clasp: On a comfortable length of thread, pick up 12 11ºs. Working in flat peyote stitch, stitch 12 rows. Zip the ends together to form a tube, and exit one end of the tube. Pick up an 8º and an 11º, skip the 11º, and sew back through the 8º to the other end of the tube. Pick up an 8º and an 11º, skip the 11º, and sew back into the tube. Work back and forth through the tube to reinforce the end beads. Work the needle to the middle of the tube, exiting a center bead of a row. Work ladder stitch two 11ºs wide for five stitches. Attach to one end of the necklace. End the thread.

33 At the other end of the necklace, attach a new thread and pick up 22 11ºs. Sew through one of the end beads on the necklace to make a loop. Reinforce the loop. End the thread in the beadwork.

GOING BAROQUE WITH PEARLS
Bracelet

Baroque pearls are my favorite type of pearl. The iridescent bronze color is a bonus that will look beautiful in your jewelry wardrobe!

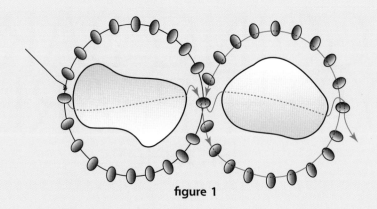

figure 1

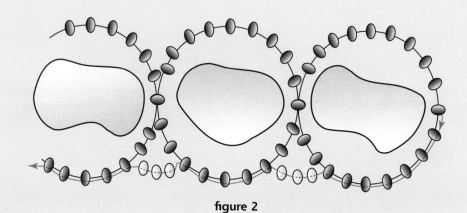

figure 2

MATERIALS

Bracelet, 8 in. (20cm) including clasp

19 bronze baroque or potato pearls, approximately 6x8mm each

4 grams 11º smoky gold bronze metallic seed beads

1 gram 11º gold metallic seed beads

1 gram 15º gold metallic seed beads

Beading thread

Needle

Scissors

STITCH

Modified daisy chain 1, p. 42

BRACELET

Begin Modified Daisy Chain 1

1 Thread a needle with 5 ft. (1.52m) of thread. Pick up 20 11º bronze metallic seed beads, and tie the beads into a circle, leaving an 8-in. (20cm) tail. Sew through the first 11º bronze again.

2 Pick up a 6x8mm pearl. Sew through the 11º bronze directly across from the 11º bronze exited in step 1.

3 Pick up 19 11º bronzes. Sew through the first 11º bronze again to make a circle.

4 Repeat steps 2 and 3 14 times, and then repeat step 2, for a total of 16 pearls **(figure 1)**.

5 After adding the last pearl, sew through seven 11º bronzes.

6 Pick up three 11º bronzes, and sew through the five center 11º bronzes in the previous circle to make a three-bead bridge. Repeat for the length of the bracelet **(figure 2)**. Sew through the 11º bronzes in the end circle to reach the other side. Repeat this step, sewing through five 11º bronzes in the end circle when you reach the other end.

7 Sew through the next five 11º bronzes, exiting the third 11º bronze from the end center 11º bronze of an end circle.

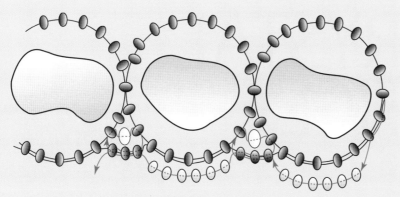

figure 3

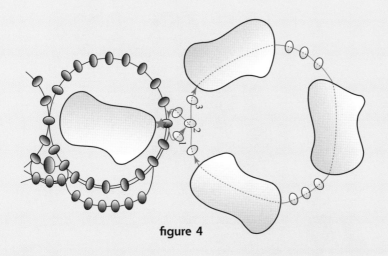

figure 4

a

b

8 Pick up six 15º gold seed beads. Sew through the next three-bead bridge and the third 11º bronze from where the circles join in the next circle. Pick up an 11º gold seed bead. Sew through the 11º bronze in the previous circle directly opposite, and sew back through the three-bead bridge. Repeat step 8 for the length of the bracelet **(figure 3)**.

9 When you reach the end circle, pick up six 15ºs and sew through five 11º bronzes.

10 Repeat step 8 on the other side of the bracelet. When you reach the last circle, sew through three 11º bronzes and exit the center 11º bronze of the circle.

11 Pick up three 11º bronzes, a pearl, three 11º bronzes, a pearl, three 11º bronzes, a pearl, and an 11º bronze. Sew through the second 11º bronze at the beginning of this step. Pick up an 11º bronze, and sew back through the starting 11º bronze on the last circle. Repeat the thread path to reinforce, and end the thread **(figure 4 and photo a)**.

12 At the other end of the bracelet, thread the tail, exit the center bead of the circle, and make a loop of 11º bronzes (approximately 24) that will fit over the button formed in step 11. Reinforce and end the thread **(photo b)**.

CRYSTAL LATTICE
Bracelet and Earrings

Stitch pairs of crystals dancing up a ladder of gold. For a shorter version, omit a row or two of crystals.

MATERIALS

**Bracelet, 9 in. (23cm)
including clasp**

28 6mm bicone crystals

10 grams 11º gold seed beads

2 grams 8º gold seed beads

2 gold jump rings

Toggle clasp

Earrings, 1¼ in. (3.2cm)

4 6mm bicone crystals

2 grams 11º gold seed beads

1 gram 8º gold seed beads

2 4mm gold jump rings

Pair of earring findings

Both

Beading thread

Needle

Scissors

2 pairs of chainnose pliers

STITCH

Modified daisy chain 2, p. 45

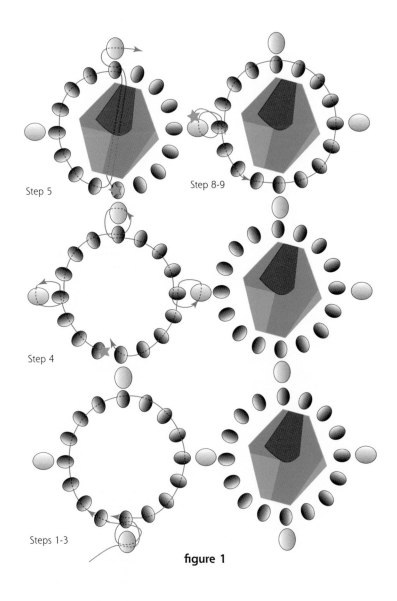

Step 5

Step 8-9

Step 4

Steps 1-3

figure 1

BRACELET

Begin Modified Daisy Chain 2

1 Pick up an 8º gold seed bead.

2 Pick up an 11º gold seed bead, and sew through the 8º and 11º again.

3 Pick up 15 11ºs. Sew through the first 11º again **(figure 1, steps 1–3)**.

4 Sew through the next four 11ºs in the circle. Pick up an 8º, and sew it to the last 11º exited **(figure 1, step 4)**. Repeat twice around the circle of beads, and sew through the next four 11ºs, exiting the first 11º exited in this step.

5 Pick up a 6mm crystal. Sew through the 11º directly opposite (the one connected to the 8º). Sew through all the 11ºs on one side of the circle back to the starting point, and sew through the crystal again. Sew through the 11º and the 8º to complete one crystal–bead circle **(figure 1, step 5)**.

6 Repeat steps 2–5 13 times.

Make the Second Side

7 Sew through the 11°s on the last crystal–bead circle to reach a side 8°.

8 Pick up an 11°, and sew it to the 8°.

9 Pick up 15 11°s. Sew back through the 11° exited at the start of this step **(figure 1, steps 8 and 9)**.

10 Sew through the next four 11°s in the circle. Pick up an 8°, and sew it to the last 11° exited. Repeat twice. Exit the 11° bead below the last 8°.

11 Pick up a crystal, and sew through the opposite 11° (the one connected to the 8°). Sew through all the 11°s on one side of the circle back to the starting point, and sew through the crystal again. Sew through the 11° and the 8°.

12 Pick up an 11°, and sew it to the 8°.

13 Pick up 15 11°s. Sew through the 11° exited at the start of this step.

14 Sew through the next four 11°s in the circle. Pick up an 8°, and sew it to the last 11° exited. Repeat three times.

When you reach the 8° on the first side of the bracelet, sew it to the corresponding 11° in the bead circle. Sew through the first 11° again.

15 Pick up a 6mm. Sew through the opposite 11° (the one connected to the 8°). Sew through all the beads on one side of the circle back to the starting point, and sew through the 6mm again. Sew through the 11° and the 8°.

16 Repeat steps 12–15 12 times to the end of the bracelet.

Add Side and Center Beads

17 Sew through the beadwork to exit an end side 8°. Position the thread to add beads between the 8°s down the side of the bracelet.

18 Pick up three 11°s, an 8°, and three 11°s. Sew through the next 8°. Repeat to the end of the bracelet.

19 Sew through the beadwork to exit an end center 8° (an 8° between the rows). Repeat step 18.

Make frequent half-hitch knots while adding the side and center beads in case the thread breaks.

20 Sew through the beadwork to the other side of the bracelet, and exit the other end side 8°. Repeat step 18.

Make End Pieces

21 Exit an end side 8°, and pick up three 11°s, an 8°, and three 11°s. Sew through the center 8° in the crystal–bead circle. Pick up three 11°s, an 8° (this is the end center 8°), and three 11°s. Sew through the next 8°. Pick up three 11°s, an 8°, and three 11°s. Sew through the next 8°. Make a half-hitch knot below the 8°, and sew back through the beads just picked up until you reach the end center 8°.

22 Pick up four 11°s, and sew through the end center 8° again to make a loop. Continue sewing through the beads to reach the 8° first exited in step 21. Make a half-hitch knot below the 8°. Repeat the thread path to the other side and back again to reinforce the end piece construction **(figure 2)**.

23 Attach a new thread at the other end of the bracelet, and repeat steps 21 and 22.

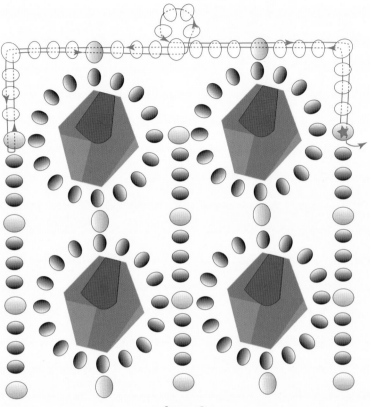

figure 2

24 Use 4mm jump rings to attach a clasp half to each of the loops created in step 22.

EARRINGS

1 For each earring: Pick up an 8º.

2 Pick up an 11º, and sew it to the 8º.

3 Pick up 15 11ºs. Sew back through the starting 11º as in step 3 of the bracelet.

4 Pick up a 6mm crystal bicone. Sew through the 11º directly opposite. Sew through all the beads on one side of the circle back to the starting point, and sew through the 6mm again. Sew through the 11º as in step 5 of the bracelet. Pick up an 8º, and sew it to the 11º.

5 Repeat steps 2–4 once.

6 Open a jump ring, and attach it to the 8º and the loop of the earring wire. Close the jump ring.

A jump ring should fit through the hole in the 8º. If the holes in your beads are too small, sew the 8º to a jump ring or split ring and then attach it to the earring wire loop.

GOLDEN GUMDROPS
Necklace

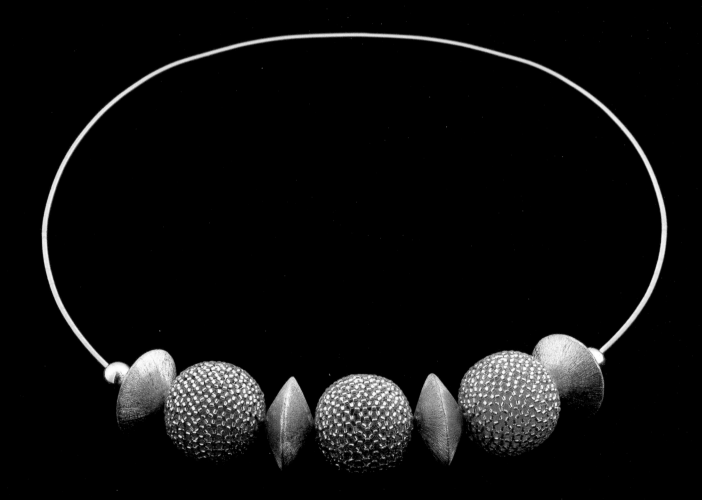

Covering a luscious resin bead in right-angle weave lets the lovely color glimmer through, tinting the gold seed beads with a subtle sheen of color.

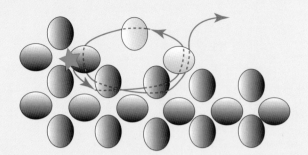

figure

MATERIALS

Necklace, 24 in. (61cm)

3 18mm or 20mm red, green, and gold round resin beads, 1 in each color

6 grams 15º gold-lined crystal seed beads

4 22x12mm brushed gold saucer beads

2 8mm round gold beads

24-in. neck wire that will fit through the bead holes

Beading thread to match the resin bead colors

Double-sided transparent tape (optional)

Toothpick (optional)

Needle

Scissors

STITCHES

Flat and tubular right-angle weave, p. 92

Place a toothpick in the bead hole on the beaded half of the sphere to keep the beads from sliding as you bead the other half.

NECKLACE

1 Begin making a covered resin bead: Work a strip of flat right-angle weave with 15º gold-lined crystal seed beads three stitches wide and as long as necessary to go around the equator of an 18–20mm resin bead. Leave room for one last stitch to fit it around the bead.

2 Cut a strip of double-sided tape in half lengthwise and stick it around the bead equator. Position the bead strip from step 1 over the tape. The tape will help hold the bead strip in place as the last stitch connects the beginning and end of the "bead belt."

3 Work the needle to one side of the bead belt. Start a new row of tubular right-angle weave along the edge of the belt. Continue working in tubular right-angle weave around the belt, decreasing as needed to keep the 15ºs flush to the resin bead. Depending on the beads and how snugly the belt fits, it might be necessary to decrease once or twice or not at all on the first row. To decrease in right-angle weave, sew through the next two beads before picking up the additional beads for the stitch **(figure)**. It will take only one bead to

complete the last stitch in the row. Once you have completed the first row, step up and start a new row around the belt. Continue in tubular right-angle weave, decreasing as necessary, until you reach the bead hole. Most rows will need one or more decreases. The last row before the hole is usually a decrease on every stitch. Finally, sew through the top bead of each stitch and pull together snugly to make a ring around the hole. Inserting a toothpick will help create a neat, tight ring. Sew through the 15ºs around the ring several times to secure it.

4 Work the needle to the other side of the belt, or attach a new thread. Complete the other half of the bead as in step 3. Remove the double-sided tape from the bead after one or two rows on this half.

5 Repeat steps 1–4 twice for a total of three covered resin beads.

6 On the neck wire, string an 8mm round gold bead, a saucer bead, and a covered resin bead. Alternate saucers and covered resin beads, finishing with a saucer and an 8mm. (If the neck wire has a clasp, remove one side of the clasp, string the beads, and reattach the clasp.)

IT'S A STITCH
Bracelet

A mix of beads in unusual colors and shapes make this bracelet fun to stitch and wear.

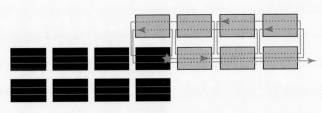

figure

MATERIALS

Bracelet, 8 in. (20cm) including clasp

10 grams 3mm rose gold iris hex beads

2 grams 8º metallic bronze iris seed beads

2 5mm gold split rings

4mm gold jump ring

Lobster claw clasp

Beading thread or Fireline

Needle

Scissors

2 pairs of chainnose pliers

STITCH

Square stitch, p. 91

BRACELET

1 On a comfortable length of thread, pick up four 3mm rose gold iris hex beads, and square stitch with hex beads back to the beginning. Leave a 6-in. (15cm) tail. Sew through the original row of hex beads, exiting opposite the tail thread. The beads in line with the tail thread are the Main Line.

2 Pick up three hex beads. Working on the side of the Main Line of hex beads opposite the previous set of square stitch hex beads picked up, square stitch back four stitches, adding a hex bead to the previous set of square stitches. Sew through the Main Line hex beads **(figure)**.

3 Repeat step 2 until the bracelet is 7 in. (18cm) long. Each additional unit of hex beads is on the opposite side of the Main Line from the previous set.

4 Square stitch a hex bead to the last hex bead on the bracelet, making a vertical stack of three hex beads. Repeat at the other end of the bracelet.

5 Sewing through the hex beads on one side of the bracelet, sew three 8º bronze seed beads between each set of hex beads for the length of the bracelet. Repeat on the other side of the bracelet **(photo)**.

6 Sew a split ring to each end of the bracelet.

7 Use a jump ring to attach a lobster claw clasp on one end.

RUSSIAN SPLENDOR
Necklace

Russian spiral and
double St. Petersburg chain
combine to make a splendid
necklace in bronze and gold,
reflecting the luxurious jewelry
of the old Russian court.
Wear it as a lariat-style
necklace tied in a square
knot at your neckline.

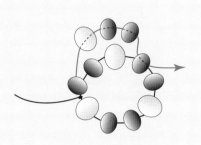

figure 1

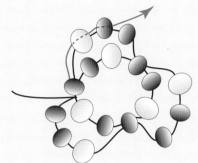

figure 2

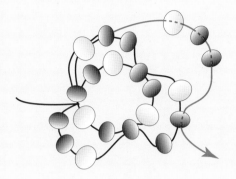

figure 3

MATERIALS

Necklace, 33 in. (84cm)

2 14mm pearls

6 8mm pearls

6 6mm pearls

28 grams 8º gold seed beads

30 grams 11º bronze seed beads

Beading thread

Needle

Scissors

Bobbin or small card (optional)

STITCHES

Russian spiral stitch, p. 53

St. Petersburg chain stitch, p. 94

NECKLACE

Make a Russian Spiral Stitch Rope

1 On a comfortable length of thread, pick up two 11º bronze seed beads and an 8º gold seed bead, leaving an 8-in. (20cm) tail. Repeat twice for a total of nine beads. Tie the beads into a circle, and sew through the first 11º picked up.

2 Pick up an 8º and two 11ºs, skip the next two beads in the previous circle (an 11º and an 8º), and sew through the next 11º. Pull snug so the new loops rest on top of the previous row to form a rope **(figure 1)**.

3 Repeat step 2 twice. Finish the first round by sewing through the first 11º.

4 Sew through the first 8º and 11º picked up in step 2. This is the step up to the next row. Pull snug **(figure 2)**.

5 Repeat steps 2–4 **(figure 3)** for 24 in. (61cm) or the desired length.

6 Sew through all the beads at the end of the rope and pull snug. Then sew through only the 8ºs on the last row two or three times, pulling snug.

7 Bridge the thread across the end of the rope by sewing from one 8º to an 8º on the opposite side of the rope twice. Make a half-hitch knot in the center of the thread bridge, and end the threads.

8 Repeat steps 6 and 7 at the other end of the rope, using the thread tail.

Make Double St. Petersburg Chain Tassels

9 On a slightly longer length of thread than usual, slide a stop bead to the center. If desired, wrap the thread tail around a bobbin or small card to keep it out of the way.

10 Work St. Petersburg chain stitch for 12 stitches. Use 11ºs for the base and use 8ºs for the accent beads in steps 3, 4, 6, and 7 on p. 94. Secure the thread and remove the needle.

11 Remove the stop bead, and thread the needle with the thread tail.

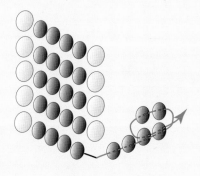

figure 4

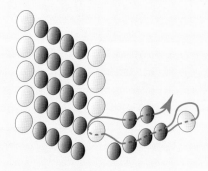

figure 5

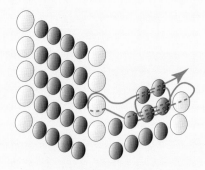

figure 6

a

b

12 Pick up six 11ºs, and sew through the third and fourth 11ºs, pushing the beads up **(figure 4)**.

13 Pick up an 8º, and sew back through three 11ºs.

14 Sew through an 8º on the completed chain and the two top 11ºs picked up in step 12 **(figure 5)**.

15 Pick up four 11ºs, and sew through the first two 11ºs again. Pick up an 8º, and sew through the three adjacent 11ºs. Sew through the next 8º in the completed chain and through the two top 11ºs picked up in this step **(figure 6)**.

16 Repeat step 15 for the length of the chain.

Finishing

17 Exit the center 8º on the wide end of the chain. Pick up an 11º, an 8mm pearl, a 6mm pearl, an 8º, and an 11º. Skip the last 11º, and sew through all the beads to the chain. Sew through the 8º on the chain, and secure the thread. Sew through all the beads in the pearl dangle again to reinforce. End the thread in the chain **(photo a)**.

18 Repeat steps 9–17 to make a chain 14 stitches long.

19 Repeat steps 9–17 to make a chain 16 stitches long.

20 Connect the three chains at the ends opposite the pearl dangles by sewing through the two 11ºs on each chain. Pull into a tight circle. Reinforce by sewing through the 11ºs again.

21 Pick up an 8º, a 14mm pearl, and an 8º. Attach to one end of the rope, using the thread bridge to center the tassel. Pull snug, and secure to the rope with a half-hitch knot. Sew through all the beads in this step again to reinforce, securing the thread in the rope and in the chains, to finish the tassel. End the threads **(photo b)**.

22 Repeat steps 9–21 to make a second tassel, and attach it to the other end of the rope.

TWISTED HERRINGBONE
Necklace

Make this stylish necklace with an easy twisted herringbone rope. Attach a large donut with a peyote stitch lark's head knot.

As a 15º is smaller than an 11º, it will start lagging behind its partner in the herringbone column. Occasionally, pick up two 15ºs instead of one to even up the column. Be sure to sew through both 15ºs at the step-up.

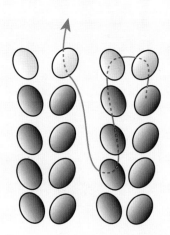

figure 1

MATERIALS

Necklace, 19 in. (48cm) including clasp

34mm black donut with off-center hole

23 grams 11º black seed beads

3 grams 11º gold seed beads

5 grams 15º gold seed beads

2 5mm gold jump rings

Clasp

Beading thread

Needle

Scissors

2 pairs of chainnose pliers

Lightweight cardboard for support (optional)

STITCHES

Tubular peyote stitch, p. 90

Tubular herringbone stitch, p. 91

NECKLACE
Make the Rope

1 On a comfortable length of thread, pick up a 15º gold seed bead and seven 11º black seed beads. Tie the beads into a circle. Sew through the 15º again.

2 Work tubular herringbone stitch for three rounds, picking up a 15º as the first bead of each round.

3 On row 5, work tubular herringbone; however, on the last stitch of the round, sew down through three 11º blacks instead of just one and up through the top 15º on the adjacent column. This starts the twist in the necklace (**figure 1**).

4 Repeat step 3 until the necklace is 17½ in. (43cm) long.

5 On the next two rounds at the step up, sew down through two 11º blacks and up through the top 15º.

figure 2

a

b

6 On the next two rounds at the step up, sew down through an 11º black and up through the top 15º.

7 On the next three rounds at the step up, sew down through an 11º black and up through the top *two* 15ºs.

8 Sew through all of the 11º blacks on the end of the rope, and pull together snugly to make a blunt end like the starting end. Repeat to reinforce.

9 Exiting one of the 11º blacks, make a small loop of four 11º blacks bridging from one side of the rope end to the other. End the thread in the rope. Repeat at the other end.

Make the Lark's Head Knot Pendant

10 Refer to **figure 2**, flipping the chart 90 degrees so it lies horizontally rather than vertically. Pick up the first two rows of gold 11ºs and black 11ºs according to the chart, working from left to right, bottom to top **(figure 2)**. Be careful: The gold segments are irregular. Tie the beads into a circle. Place the bead circle around a lightweight piece of cardboard rolled to fit inside. Tape the cardboard overlap securely.

11 Working in tubular peyote, follow the chart to make a long, wide ring.

12 Remove the ring from the cardboard tube. Fold the ring in half. String the donut on the folded ring **(photo a)**.

13 Pull one end of the ring through the other to make a lark's head knot **(photo b)**.

14 String the pendant on the rope. Use 4mm jump rings to attach a clasp half to each end bead loop.

CAGED CRYSTALS
Bracelet

Intricate filigree beadwork traps a flat, round crystal inside a lacy square cage. The fire-polished bead-studded sides add more bling to the bracelet. The three-dimensional shape of the cage may be a challenge!

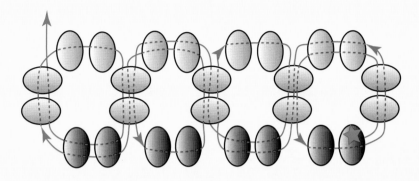

figure 1

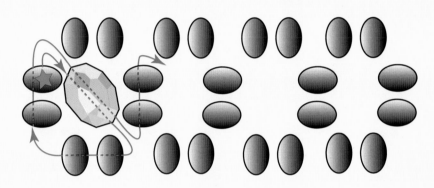

figure 2

MATERIALS

Bracelet, 8½ in. (21.6cm) including clasp

7 16mm crystal rivolis or similar pressed-glass beads

114 3mm round crystal fire-polished beads

10 grams 11º gold seed beads

Beading thread

Needle

Scissors

STITCHES

Even-count flat peyote stitch, p. 89

Ladder stitch, p. 90

Flat right-angle weave stitch, p. 92

When working with more than one bead per side in right-angle weave, sew through each side separately rather than trying to gather two or more at a time onto the needle. The shape will stay a bit more square and you'll be able to check that each side has the proper number of beads as you stitch. Be careful: Right-angle weave is difficult to fix if you make an error and don't catch it right away!

BRACELET

Make the Bottom

1 On a comfortable length of thread, pick up eight 11º gold seed beads. Tie the 11ºs into a circle. Work a strip of flat right-angle weave four stitches wide by four stitches long. Use two 11ºs per side instead of one to create open squares. This completes the bottom of the rivoli cage.

Make Side Walls

2 Exiting the last 11º on an outside edge of the bottom, pick up six 11ºs. Sew back through the two bottom 11ºs, the 11ºs just picked up, and the two edge 11ºs on the next stitch of the bottom. Continue working right-angle weave across the bottom edge **(figure 1, side view)**.

3 At the end of this side of the bottom, exit the side 11ºs just picked up. To turn the corner, pick up four 11ºs. Sew through the edge 11ºs of the first stitch of the bottom row, the side 11ºs of the last stitch, the 11ºs just picked up, and the edge 11ºs of the next stitch of the bottom. Remember to continue alternating the direction of each stitch.

figure 3

figure 4

4 Continue working right-angle weave stitches around the bottom. Use four 11ºs for each stitch except the last stitch (use two 11ºs to finish) **(photo a)**.

Add Side Wall Beads
5 Exiting the top 11º of a side stitch, pick up a 3mm round fire-polished bead. Sew through the two 11ºs at the bottom of the right-angle weave stitch and back up to the first 11º exited in this step. Sew through the 3mm again, and then sew through the side 11ºs of the next stitch. Continue adding 3mms in the side walls. Avoid sewing through any of the 11ºs on the top of the side wall **(figure 2, side view)**.

Make the Enclosure Row on Top
6 Work the needle to exit the top side 11º at a corner of a side wall.

7 Use the last stitch on this row and the first stitch around the corner plus four 11ºs to make a right-angle weave stitch as shown **(figure 3, top view)**. The stitch will have sides from the top of each side wall row and the four 11ºs just picked up. It will fold inward from the side walls to form an inside row. Sew through the top 11ºs of the next stitch **(figure 3)**.

8 Work two right-angle weave stitches. At the corner, use 11ºs from each side plus two additional 11ºs to turn the corner. Each stitch will have eight 11ºs, although the shape of each stitch will vary as you work. Remember, each

stitch alternates direction. The last stitch will only need two 11ºs. There will be 12 stitches in the enclosure row. Exit to the inside of the row **(photo b)**.

9 Slide the rivoli into the cage under the enclosure row, lifting the edges as needed.

10 Sew through all the top 11ºs in the right-angle weave stitches on the inside edge of the row (16 11ºs), pulling snug to form a ring. Repeat to tighten and reinforce. End the thread. The rivoli will be loose inside the cage, and the cage will feel soft.

11 Repeat steps 1–10 six times for a total of seven rivoli cages.

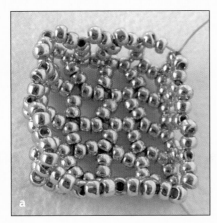

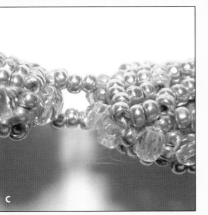

End the threads and attach new threads to the bottom of the beadwork.

Finish the Bracelet

12 Attach a thread to the back of a cage. Sew up through two center 11ºs on one side. Pick up three 11ºs, and sew down through the corresponding stack of center beads on another cage.

13 Pick up three 11ºs, and sew up through the starting center 11ºs on the other cage. Pull the two cages together snugly. Repeat the thread path to reinforce the 11º bridges between the two cages. Repeat for each cage until all seven cages are attached **(figure 4 and photo c)**.

14 Attach a thread to the end of the bracelet. Make a loop of seven 11ºs by sewing vertically through the center stack of 11ºs. Reinforce, and end the thread. Repeat at the other end of the bracelet.

15 Make the toggle: Using 11ºs, work a strip of flat peyote 12 beads wide and 12 rows long. Zip the ends together to make a tube. Sew a 3mm on each end of the tube using the threads between the 11ºs on the end. Work the needle to the center of the tube. Make a ladder strip two beads wide by six stitches long with 11ºs to finish the toggle.

16 Exiting the 11ºs in the last ladder stitch, pick up five 11ºs. Sew through the loop of 11ºs created in step 14 on one end of the bracelet. Sew back through the last ladder stitch to make a loop of 11ºs, and attach the toggle to the bracelet. Reinforce the loop, and end the threads **(photo d)**.

17 On a new thread, pick up 28 11ºs and sew through the loop at the other end of the bracelet and back through all the 11ºs picked up to make a circle. Repeat the thread path to reinforce, and end the thread with half-hitch knots between the 11ºs in the circle.

CROWNED
Pendant

MATERIALS

Necklace, 21 in. (53cm) including clasp

27mm fuchsia rivoli

6 grams 8º bronze metallic iris seed beads

15 grams 11º bronze metallic iris seed beads

3 grams 11º dark gold seed beads

1 yd. (.9m) 2mm brown satin rattail cord

2 4mm gold split rings

2 4mm gold jump rings

Hook-and-eye clasp

Beading thread

Needle

Scissors

2 pairs of chainnose pliers

STITCHES

Tubular and circular right-angle weave, p. 92 and 93

Modified herringbone stitch, p. 63

You'll wear this splendid crowned pendant in dark golds and fuchsias with a regal attitude.

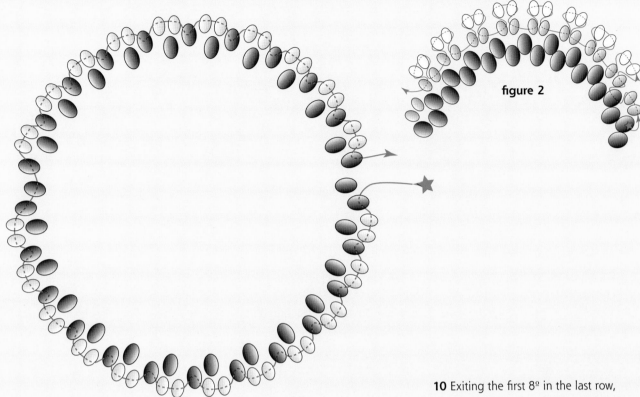

figure 1

figure 2

NECKLACE
Make the Pendant
1 On a comfortable length of thread, pick up six 8º bronze seed beads. Tie the 11ºs into a circle. Sew through the first 11º picked up.

2 Work a right-angle weave increase stitch with 8ºs on each bead in step 1. The finished row will have 12 8ºs on the outer edge. Step up to start the new row.

3 Work right angle weave with 8ºs. Increase on every other bead in step 2. The finished row will have 18 8ºs. Step up to start the new row.

4 Work right-angle weave with 8ºs. Increase on every third 8º in step 3. The finished row will have 24 8ºs. Step up to start the new row.

5 Work right-angle weave on every 8º in step 4 with 11º bronze seed beads. The finished row will have 24 11º bronzes. Step up to start the new row.

6 Repeat step 5.

7 Center a 27mm rivoli in the beadwork.

8 Sew a 11º bronze between each 11º bronze picked up in step 6. Pull snug. Repeat the thread path to reinforce and tighten.

Make the Edge Trim
9 Exiting the last row of 8ºs (step 4), work clockwise to sew a 8º between each 8º on this row. Step up.

For more stitch direction, follow the instructions in the Basics section for circular right-angle weave.

10 Exiting the first 8º in the last row, pick up two 11º dark gold seed beads, and sew through the next 8º. Repeat 11 times for a total of 12 11ºs. Skip picking up one pair of 11º dark golds, and then continue picking up two 11º dark golds 10 times. You will have two 11º dark golds between each 8º, with matching gaps on each side of the pendant **(figure 1)**.

Add the Top Crown
11 Exiting the 8º, sew back through the last two 11º dark golds picked up and the next 8º. Sew through the next 11º dark gold.

12 Pick up two 11º dark golds. Sew through the next two 11º dark golds. Repeat seven times for a total of eight pairs of 11º dark golds. After the last pair, only sew through one 11º dark gold **(figure 2)**.

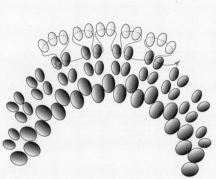

figure 3

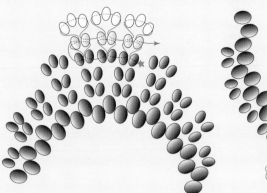

figure 4

figure 5

13 Work the needle to the first 11º dark gold of the third column in the row just picked up. Pick up three 11º dark golds, and sew through the next two 11º dark golds.

14 Pick up two 11º dark golds, and sew through the next 11º dark gold.

15 Pick up two 11º dark golds, and sew through the next 11º dark gold, placing the pair of 11º dark golds between the two columns of 11º dark golds.

16 Pick up two 11º dark golds, and sew through the next two 11º dark golds.

17 Pick up three 11º dark golds, and sew through the next 11º dark gold **(figure 3)**.

18 Work the needle to the top of the previous column of 11º dark golds.

19 Pick up two gold beads, and sew through the next two 11º dark golds. Repeat once. Pick up two 11º dark golds, and sew through the next 11º dark gold **(figure 4)**.

20 Sew back through the last 11º dark

gold picked up. Pick up three 11º dark golds. Sew through the next two 11º dark golds. Repeat once. Pick up three 11º dark golds, and sew through the next 11º dark gold. End the thread.

Add the Bottom Crown
21 Attach a thread, exiting the first 11º dark gold of the fifth pair from the gap left in step 10.

22 Pick up two 11º dark golds. Sew through the next two 11º dark golds. Repeat twice. Pick up two 11º dark golds and sew through the next 11º dark gold. These four columns will be directly opposite the bead crown added at the top of the pendant **(figure 5)**.

23 Sew back through the last 11º dark gold picked up. Pick up two 11º dark golds, and sew through the next two 11º dark golds.

24 Pick up three 11º dark golds, and sew through the next two 11º dark golds. Repeat.

25 Pick up two 11º dark golds, and sew through the next 11º dark gold. End the thread.

Make the Rope
26 Using 11º bronzes, work four stitches of right-angle weave. Wrap the 11º bronzes around the cord. Connect the ends with a fifth stitch to create one row of tubular right-angle weave.

27 Using 11º dark golds, work two rows of tubular right-angle weave.

28 Using 8ºs, work three rows of tubular right-angle weave.

29 Using 11º dark golds, work two rows of tubular right-angle weave.

30 Using 11º bronzes, work tubular right-angle weave until the total length of the beaded rope is 9 in. (23cm). Trim the cord to fit the rope. Sew a split ring to the end of the rope.

31 Repeat steps 26–30 for the other side of the necklace.

Assemble the Necklace
32 Attach one rope to the pendant using the gap in the pendant trim and the two exposed 8ºs to secure it. Flatten the rope slightly to get a good fit. Repeat on the other side.

33 Using jump rings, attach a clasp half to each split ring.

JEWELED RINGS
Necklace and Earrings

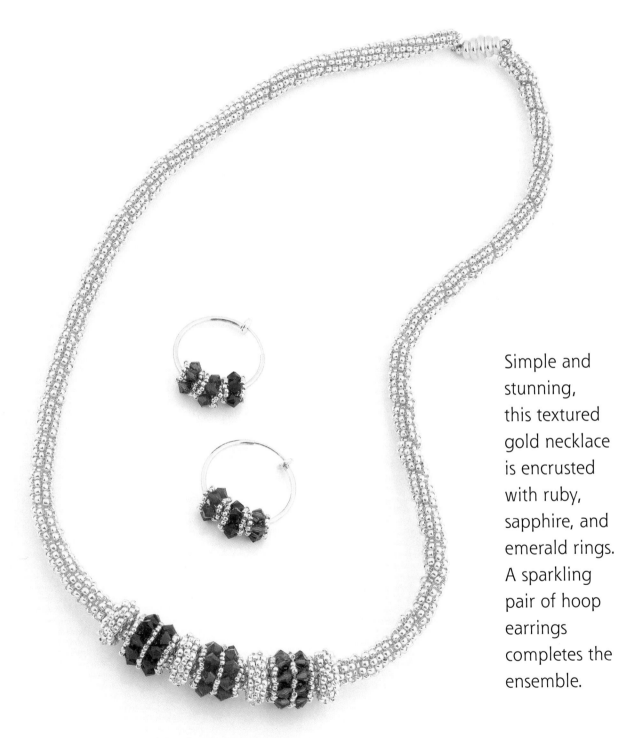

Simple and stunning, this textured gold necklace is encrusted with ruby, sapphire, and emerald rings. A sparkling pair of hoop earrings completes the ensemble.

MATERIALS

Necklace, 24 in. (61cm) including clasp

18 4mm emerald bicone crystals

18 4mm sapphire bicone crystals

18 4mm ruby bicone crystals

22 grams 11º gold seed beads

7 grams 15º gold seed beads

30 in. (76cm) 1mm gold satin rattail cord

30 in. .019mm flexible gold beading wire

13x8mm magnetic swirl clasp

2 3–4mm gold jump rings

2 gold crimp beads

2 pairs of chainnose pliers

Crimping pliers

Wire cutters

Earrings, 1⅛ in. (2.9cm)

10 4mm emerald bicone crystals

10 4mm sapphire bicone crystals

10 4mm ruby bicone crystals

2 grams 15º gold seed beads

Pair 1-in. (2.5cm) gold hoop earring findings

Both

Beading thread

Needle

Scissors

STITCHES

Odd-count flat and odd-count tubular peyote stitch, p. 89 and 90

Flat right-angle weave stitch, p. 92

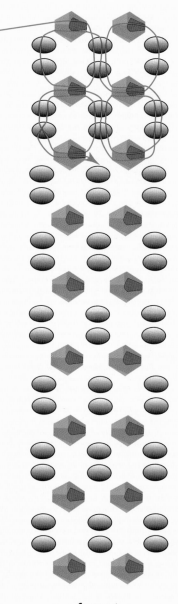

figure 1

NECKLACE

Begin the Necklace Rope

1 On a comfortable length of thread, pick up a 15º gold seed bead and eight 11º gold seed beads. Tie the beads into a circle around the 1mm gold satin cord. Picking up the same type of bead that you are exiting each time, work odd-count tubular peyote stitch for 23 in. (58cm) to make a rope.

2 Thread the flexible gold beading wire through the rope. Do not trim the excess wire, as you will use it later to attach the clasp.

3 On one end of the rope, sew through the satin cord and the rope several times to secure the cord inside. Trim the cord even with the end of the rope.

4 Decrease the end of the rope by one bead each row until three beads remain. To decrease, instead of picking up a new bead to make the next stitch, leave the space empty and sew through the next bead.

5 Sew through all three beads and pull snug. End the thread in the rope.

6 Repeat steps 3–5 at the other end of the rope.

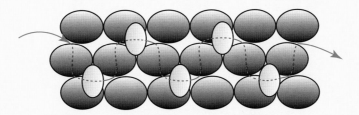

figure 2

Make Jeweled Rings

7 On a new length of thread, pick up a 4mm emerald bicone crystal, two 15ºs, a 4mm emerald, and two 15ºs. Tie the beads into a circle. Sew through the first 4mm emerald picked up and the next two 15ºs.

8 Using 15ºs and the 4mm emeralds, make a strip of flat right-angle weave two stitches wide by eight stitches long as shown **(figure 1)**.

9 Attach the ends of the strip together, using 15ºs to complete the stitches between the 4mm emeralds, to make a ring.

10 Sew a 15º between each pair of 15ºs on the sides of the ring.

11 Repeat steps 7–10 with 4mm sapphire bicone crystals and 4mm ruby bicone crystals.

Make Gold Rings

12 Using 11ºs, stitch a flat odd-count peyote strip three stitches wide by 28 rows long (14 11ºs on each side). Zip up the ends to make a ring.

13 Sew a 15º between each pair of 11ºs on the sides of the ring.

14 Exiting one of the center 11ºs, pick up a 15º. Sew through the next 11º center bead and repeat, zigzagging along each side of the center beads to finish the ring **(figure 2)**.

15 Repeat steps 12–14 three times for a total of four gold rings.

16 Slide the completed rings on the rope, alternating gold rings and jeweled rings.

17 Attach a jump ring to each half of the clasp.

18 String a crimp bead and a jump ring on the beading wire. Pass the wire back through the crimp bead, and crimp. Trim the excess wire. Repeat at the other end of the necklace.

EARRINGS

1 Work a strip of flat right-angle weave one stitch wide by four stitches long. Start by picking up a 4mm bicone crystal, two 15ºs, a 4mm, and two 15ºs. For each subsequent stitch, use two 15ºs, a 4mm, and two 15ºs. Make sure the strip will fit around the hoop before using 15ºs to connect the end and make a ring.

2 Stitch a 15º between each pair of 15ºs on the sides of the ring.

3 Make two rings of each crystal color.

4 Slide one ring of each color on a hoop earring. Repeat to make a second earring.

DRAGON PEARLS
Necklace and Earrings

These shapes remind me of dragon's claws clutching pearls—a fitting accompaniment for a regal outfit!

MATERIALS

Necklace, 25 in. (64cm) including clasp

- 10 14mm pearls
- 2 8mm round gold beads
- 2 7mm round gold beads
- 2 6mm round gold beads
- 30 grams 11º gold one-cut seed beads
- 10 grams 15º light bronze seed beads
- 30 in. (76cm) .019 flexible gold beading wire
- Pearl-trimmed box clasp
- 2 gold crimp beads
- 2 5mm gold split rings
- 2 5mm gold jump rings
- Crimping pliers
- Support (optional)

Earrings, 1½ in. (3.8cm)

- 2 14mm pearls
- 2 grams 11º gold one-cut seed beads
- 2 11º bronze seed beads
- 1 gram 15º light bronze seed beads
- 2 3–4mm gold jump rings
- Pair of gold earring posts
- 2 3-in. (7.6cm) gold headpins
- Roundnose pliers

Both

- Beading thread
- Needles
- Scissors
- 2 pairs of chainnose pliers
- Wire cutter

STITCH

Modified tubular herringbone stitch, p. 69

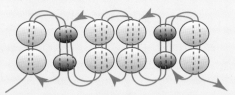

figure 1

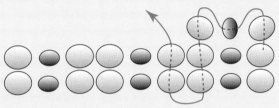

figure 2

NECKLACE

Make Flared Bead Tubes Using Modified Tubular Herringbone Stitch

1 On a comfortable length of thread, make a two-drop ladder: *Make a two-bead stack of 11º gold seed beads, a two-bead stack of 15º bronze seed beads, and a two-bead stack of 11ºs **(figure 1)**. Repeat from * four times for a total of 15 bead stacks. Join the ends to make a circle. Work the needle to exit a stack of 11ºs.

2 Pick up an 11º, a 15º, and an 11º. Sew down through the next 11º bead stack and up through the adjacent 11º bead stack **(figure 2)**. Repeat around the circle to start the modified herringbone stitch. Step up at the end of the round.

> In step 2, I prefer to sew completely through the ladder column to work the herringbone stitch rather than wiggling my needle between the two stacked beads. For all subsequent rows, I sew through only one bead in the column.

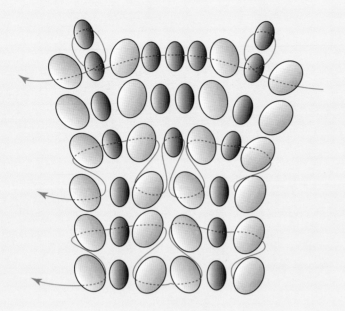

figure 3

String the Necklace

12 On the flexible gold beading wire, string a pearl and long tube, and then alternate pearls and short tubes. Finish with a pearl, a long tube, and a pearl.

13 On each end, string an 8mm gold bead, a 7mm gold bead, a 6mm gold bead, a crimp, and a split ring. Pass the beading wire back through the crimp. Crimp, and trim the excess wire.

14 Use a jump ring to attach a clasp half to each end of the necklace.

EARRINGS

1 For each earring: Follow steps 1 and 2 of the necklace, and then make the flared end following steps 5–8.

2 Attach a thread to the two-drop ladder of beads exiting on the other side. Work one round of herringbone (step 2) and then follow step 3 for 6 rounds.

3 Taper one end: Exiting a 15º, sew a 11º between each 15º. Step up through the first 11º picked up in this row. Pull snug.

4 Exit an 11º, and sew a 15º between each 11º to finish the earring tube. Pull snug. Repeat the thread path to reinforce, and end the threads.

5 On a headpin, string an 11º bronze seed bead, a 14mm pearl, and the earring tube. Use roundnose pliers to make a small loop on the end of the headpin, and trim the excess wire.

6 Use a jump ring to attach the headpin to an earring post.

3 Pick up an 11º, a 15º, and an 11º. Sew through the next two 11ºs. Repeat around the circle of beads. Step up at the end of the round. The 15º "floats" between the 11ºs in the herringbone column **(figure 3, bottom round)**.

4 Repeat step 3 for 15 rounds.

5 Pick up an 11º, a 15º, and an 11º. These are the beads for the normal stitch. Sew through the next 11º. Pick up a 15º, and sew through the next 11º. (This starts the flare by placing a 15º between two normal stitches.) Repeat around the circle of beads **(figure 3, middle round)**. Step up at the end of the round.

6 Repeat step 5, using two 15ºs instead of one 15º in the flare stitch.

7 Repeat step 5, using three 15ºs instead of one 15º in the flare stitch.

8 After the step up at the end of the round, sew through the beadwork to a 15º in a normal stitch column (the floating bead). Pick up a 15º, and sew it to the floating 15º at the top of the column, making a tiny claw. Follow the thread path to the next floating 15º in a normal stitch column. Repeat around the circle, and end the thread **(figure 3, top round)**.

9 Attach a thread to the two-drop ladder at the other end of the short bead tube. Repeat steps 5–8.

10 Repeat steps 1–9 six times to make a total of seven short tubes.

11 Repeat steps 1–9 (except in step 4, repeat for 68 rows instead of 15) to make two long bead tubes.

TSARINA
Necklaces and Earrings

Create lovely,
opulent Russian-
style jewelry with
a delicate touch.
Make four lacy
chains, and wear
them all together,
separately, or
attached to one
another to create a
very long necklace
that loops around
your neck many
times. Hang the
pendant from
a chain for a
finishing touch.

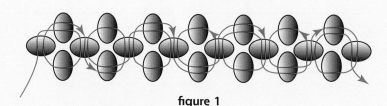
figure 1

MATERIALS

Necklace, chains 20, 22, 24, and 26 in. (51, 56, 61, and 66cm) long

16x12mm turquoise cabochon

22 grams 11º gold seed beads

3 grams 11º pearl seed beads

2 grams 11º turquoise seed beads

3 grams 11º silver-lined crystal seed beads

1 gram 15º gold seed beads

4 15x44mm tubular (bayonet-style) clasps

Earrings, 1 in. (2.5cm)

2 14x10mm turquoise cabochons

2 grams 11º gold seed beads

1 gram 11º pearl seed beads

1 gram 11º silver-line crystal seed beads

1 gram 15º gold seed beads

Pair of gold earring wires

2 4–5mm gold jump rings

2 pairs of chainnose pliers

Both

Beading thread

Needle

Scissors

STITCHES

Flat and circular right-angle weave, p. 92 and 93

> Choose the turquoise cabochons first, and then select matching seed beads. Turquoise has many color variations, from clear sky blues to sea greens.

NECKLACE

Make the Chains

1 On a comfortable length of thread, pick up four 11º gold seed beads, and begin right-angle weave: Position the first stitch so the thread tail exits the 11º gold to the left (you'll use it later to attach the clasp). Start the next stitch from the 11º gold on the right, and continue with single right-angle weave stitches for 20 in. (51cm) **(figure 1)**. Sew half of a clasp to the end.

2 Sew back through the length of the chain, sew through two 11º golds, pick up an 11º pearl seed bead, and sew diagonally through three 11º golds to the other side of the chain. Pick up an 11º turquoise seed bead. Sew diagonally through three 11º golds to the other side of the chain. Pick up an 11º silver-lined crystal seed bead, and sew through three 11º golds to the other side of the chain **(figure 2)**. Continue adding 11º pearls, 11º turquoises, and 11º crystals to the chain, sewing diagonally from one side to the other. When you reach the end, sew on the other half of the clasp. End the thread.

3 Repeat steps 1 and 2 to make three more chains 22, 24, and 26 in. (56, 61, and 66cm) long.

Make the Pendant

4 On a comfortable length of thread, pick up six 11º golds. Tie the 11º golds into a circle. Sew through the first 11º gold again.

5 Work a right-angle weave increase stitch with 11º golds on each 11º gold in step 4. The finished round will have 12 11º golds on the outer edge. Step up to start the next round.

6 Work a right-angle weave stitch with 11º golds. Increase on every other 11º gold picked up in step 5. The finished round will have 18 11º golds. Step up to start the next round.

7 Work a right-angle weave stitch with 11º golds on every 11º gold picked up in step 6. The finished round will have 18 11º golds. Step up to start the next round.

8 Work a right-angle weave stitch with 15º gold seed beads on every 11º gold picked up in step 7. The finished round will have 18 15ºs.

9 Center the cabochon on the beadwork.

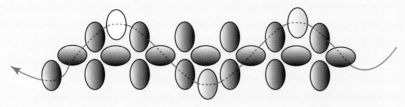

figure 2

10 Sew a 15º between each top 15º of the right-angle weave stitches picked up in step 8. Repeat the thread path through all the 15ºs. Pull the 15ºs together snugly.

11 Make trim rows: Work the needle to a top 11º on a right-weave angle stitch in step 7 (the last row of 11º golds). Sew an 11º pearl between each 11º gold in the round. Step up through the first 11º pearl at the end of the round.

12 Sew a 11º crystal between each 11º pearl in step 11.

13 Exiting an 11º gold behind the trim rows (steps 11 and 12) at the top of the cabochon, pick up an 11º pearl and 15 11º golds. Sew back through the first 11º gold picked up and the 11º pearl. Stitch into the body of the pendant to create a bead loop. Repeat the thread path to reinforce the loop.

14 Center the pendant on one of the chains.

For more stitch directions, use the instructions in the "Stitch Basics" section, p. 93, circular right-angle weave.

EARRINGS

1 For each earring: On a comfortable length of thread, pick up six 11º golds. Tie the 11º golds into a circle. Sew through the first 11º gold again.

2 Work a right-angle weave increase stitch with 11º golds on each 11º gold in step 4. The finished round will have 12 11º golds on the outer edge. Step up to start the next round.

3 Work a right-angle weave stitch with 11º golds. Increase on every other 11º gold picked up in step 5. The finished round will have 18 11º golds. Step up to start the next round.

4 Work a right-angle weave stitch with 15ºs on every 11º gold picked up in step 3. The finished round will have 18 15ºs. Step up to start the next round.

5 Work right-angle weave stitch with 15ºs on every 15º picked up in step 4. The finished round will have 18 15ºs. Step up to start the new round.

Even though the cabochon is oval and the beadwork is circular, the stretch in right-angle weave will let the beadwork fit around the stone.

6 Center the cabochon on the beadwork.

7 Sew through all the up-beads on the right-angle weave stitches in step 5. Pull snug. Repeat, pulling snugly to tighten more.

8 Make trim rows: Work the needle to a top 11º gold on the right-angle weave stitches in step 3 (the last row of 11º golds). Sew an 11º pearl between each 11º gold in the row. Step up through the first 11º pearl picked up.

9 Sew an 11º crystal between each 11º pearl picked up in step 8.

10 Exiting an 11º pearl at the top of the earring, pick up five 11º golds. Sew back through all the beads and into the body of the pendant to create a bead loop. Reinforce the loop. End the thread.

11 Use a jump ring to attach the earring loop and an earring wire.

73

METALLINI CELLINI
Bracelet

Cellini spirals are created by using different sizes of beads. Experimentation is usually required to find a set of beads that result in a smooth, attractive spiral. You'll need a minimum of four different bead sizes, but the maximum is up to you and your bead stash!

MATERIALS

Bracelet, 8½ in. (21.6cm) including clasp

25 grams 4mm round gold beads (approximately 150 beads)

10 grams 8º nickel silver seed beads

4 grams 11º nickel silver seed beads

3 grams 11º steel cylinder beads

2 5mm gold split rings

2 3–4mm gold jump rings

Toggle clasp

Fireline

Needle

Scissors

Support (optional)

2 pairs of chainnose pliers

STITCH

Odd-count tubular peyote stitch, p. 90

BRACELET

1 Pick up an 11º steel cylinder bead, two 11º nickel seed beads, two 8º nickel seed beads, two 4mm round gold beads, two 8ºs, and two 11ºs. Tie the beads into a circle. Sew through the first seed bead picked up.

2 Picking up the same type of bead that you are exiting each time, work odd-count tubular peyote for 8 in. (20cm). Working around a support is very helpful for the first inch.

3 When you reach the end, stitch two rows of 11ºs only, and then decrease two beads (one on each side of the row) every other row until only two beads are left. To decrease, do not pick up a new 11º to make the next stitch; instead just sew through the next 11º. Sew a split ring to the end of the bracelet.

4 At the other end of the bracelet, attach a new thread or use the tail thread to repeat step 3.

5 Use a jump ring to attach a clasp half to each split ring.

CAPTURED PEARLS
Bracelet

Bronze bugles, gold beads, and pearls create a rectangular cage to capture a string of pearls for a charming bracelet.

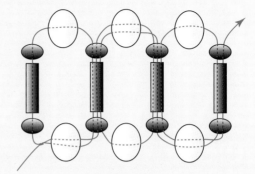

figure

MATERIALS

Bracelet, 8 in. (20cm) including clasp

2 grams size 2 bronze bugles

2 grams 6º pearl seed beads

2 grams 8º pearl seed beads

2 grams 11º dark gold silver-lined seed beads

Toggle clasp

2 5mm gold split rings

2 5mm gold jump rings

Beading thread

Needle

Scissors

2 pairs of chainnose pliers

Wooden support (optional)

STITCH

Tubular right-angle weave, p. 92

> It may be helpful to wrap the first three right-angle weave stitches around a wooden dowel before joining the ends. You can continue using the dowel for the rest of the bracelet.

BRACELET

1 On a comfortable length of thread, pick up an 8º pearl seed bead, an 11º gold seed bead, a size 2 bronze bugle bead, an 11º, an 8º, an 11º, a bugle, and an 11º. Tie the beads into a circle. Pearls will form the top and bottom of the right-angle weave stitch, with the 11º–bugle–11º sequence forming the sides. Position the tail thread at the bottom left of the circle. Exit the top 11º of the right-side 11º–bugle–11º sequence.

2 Pick up an 8º, an 11º, a bugle, an 11º, and an 8º. Sew back through the right side of the previous stitch, exiting the right-side 11º–bugle–11º sequence of this stitch. Repeat **(figure)**.

3 Join the ends of the right-angle weave stitches, using 8ºs to complete the stitch. Exit the top 8º to start a new row of tubular right-angle weave.

4 Continue working tubular right-angle weave to make a hollow rope until the bracelet is 7 in. (18cm) long.

5 Sew through the 8ºs at the end of the rope and then into the hollow center of the first right-angle weave stitch.

6 Pick up a 6º pearl seed bead, and push it through the bugles into the center of the rope. Move the needle down the interior of the rope to the center of the next right-angle weave stitch.

7 Repeat step 6 to add a 6º pearl in the center of each rectangular cage.

8 Sew through all the 8ºs at the end of the tube, and then follow the thread path back through all the center pearls to the other end.

9 Secure the thread by making a half-hitch knot around the threads between the final circle of pearls. Sew a split ring to the end of the bracelet.

10 At the other end of the bracelet, use the tail thread to sew through all the pearl beads on the end of the rectangle tube, and repeat step 9.

11 Use a jump ring to attach a clasp half to each end of the bracelet.

OVAL CHAIN LINK
Bracelet

Golden oval chain links are connected
with cobalt blue links trimmed with
gold—a beautifully rich color combination.

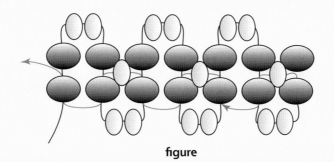

figure

BRACELET

Make Links

1 On a comfortable length of thread, using 11º gold seed beads, stitch a ladder five beads long. Connect the ends to make a ring.

2 Work tubular brick stitch for 3 in. (7.6m) (50 rows) to make a rope.

3 Insert a 3-in. piece of wire into the rope.

4 Bend the rope into an oval shape using a pencil, pen, or dowel to help round the ends. Sew the ends of the rope together.

5 Repeat steps 1–4 four times to make a total of five gold oval links.

Make Connecting Bands

6 Using 11º dark blue seed beads, stitch a two-drop ladder 20 beads long.

7 Exiting the side of the ladder, pick up two 15º gold seed beads, and sew through the next row of 11º dark blues.

8 Zigzag down the ladder band, repeating step 7 to the end of the band. You will have two 15ºs on each side of the band on every other ladder row. At the end, exit the ditch (the space between two 11º dark blues) in the center of the ladder.

9 Pick up a 15º, and sew through the 11º dark blue on the next row to the outside edge.

10 Sew through the 11º dark blue on the next row to the center ditch.

11 Repeat steps 9–10 for the length of the band, placing a 15º in the ditch every other row **(figure)**.

12 Loop the band from steps 6–11 through two gold oval links. Sew the ends of the band together. Adjust the 15º trim, if necessary, by adding any missing beads at the join.

13 Repeat steps 6–12 three times to connect the five oval gold links.

Make a Clasp Band

14 Using 11º dark blues, stitch a two-drop ladder 16 beads long.

15 Sew a clasp half to each end of the band from step 14.

16 Repeat steps 7–11 to add 15ºs to the band.

17 Use the band from steps 14–16 to connect the first and last links of the bracelet. After positioning the band to hide the clasp on the inside, stitch through the beadwork to hold it in place.

MATERIALS

Bracelet, 8 in. (20cm)

15 grams 11º gold seed beads

3 grams 11º dark blue seed beads

2 grams 15º gold seed beads

15 in. (38cm) 28-gauge gold wire

2-part 9x4mm gold magnetic clasp

Beading thread

Needle

Scissors

Wire cutters

Pencil, pen, or dowel

STITCHES

Ladder stitch, p. 90

Tubular brick stitch, p. 91

DAMASCENE FLORAL
Bracelet and Earrings

Toledo, Spain is famous for a handicraft called *damascene*. It was developed from the ancient Egyptian, Greek, and Roman art of interlacing gold on iron or steel, then firing it so the underlying material oxidizes and becomes black with the gold in sharp relief. My background is dark gray or pewter, but the effect is just as lovely.

figure 1

figure 2

MATERIALS

Bracelet, 7½ in. (19.1cm) including clasp

6 grams 11º bright gold cylinder beads

6 grams 11º dark steel cylinder beads

Earrings, 1x1¼ in. (2.5x3.2cm)

1 gram 11º bright gold cylinder beads

1 gram 11º dark steel cylinder beads

Pair of gold earring wires

2 3–4mm gold jump rings

2 pairs of chainnose pliers

Both

Beading thread

Needle

Scissors

STITCH

Even-count flat peyote stitch, p. 89

The pattern is non-repeating. You can easily adjust the length of the bracelet with additional rows of gold beads on each end before creating the clasp.

BRACELET

Make the Band

1 On a comfortable length of thread, work even-count peyote stitch using black and gold cylinder beads, following the illustration **(figure 1)**. Start at the bottom (buttonhole) end, and work left to right.

Make the Toggle

2 Pick up 16 11º gold cylinder beads. Work even-count peyote stitch for eight rows. Zip the edges to make a tube.

3 Work your needle to the center of the tube. Work a strip of even-count peyote stitch, two beads wide by four rows long. Connect the strip to the end of the bracelet.

EARRINGS

1 For each earring: Work brick stitch, following the illustration **(figure 2)**. Start with the longest row in the middle and work downward. Then work upward from the middle row to each top point.

2 Exit a top point gold cylinder, and pick up 16 gold cylinders. Attach to the other top point. Sew back through the cylinders just picked up, exiting the ninth cylinder. Pick up three gold cylinders and sew back through the ninth cylinder again to form a loop. Continue back to the starting cylinder. Reinforce.

3 Attach an earring wire and the loop with a jump ring.

ETRUSCAN
Necklace and Earrings

The Etruscans, an ancient Italic civilization, specialized in adding gold granulation to their jewelry. These beads mimic the rich, precious look.

MATERIALS

**Necklace, 19 in. (48cm)
including clasp**

- 1 18mm moonlight crystal rivoli
- 5 16mm moonlight crystal rivolis
- 4 14mm moonlight crystal rivolis
- 25 grams 11º gold seed beads
- 16 grams 15º gold seed beads
- 24 in. (61cm) 2mm white or gold satin rattail
- 2 5mm gold split rings

Earrings, 1½ in. (3.8cm)

- 2 16mm moonlight crystal rivolis
- 2 14mm moonlight crystal rivolis
- 3 grams 11º gold seed beads
- 2 grams 15º gold seed beads
- 2 5mm gold jump rings
- Pair of gold earring findings, post or wire
- 2 pairs of chainnose pliers

Both

- Beading thread
- Needles
- Scissors

STITCHES

- Flat peyote stitch, p. 90
- Tubular and circular right-angle weave stitch, p. 92 and 93

> For more stitch directions, use the instructions in the "Stitch Basics" section, p. 93, for circular right-angle weave.

NECKLACE

Make 14mm Rivoli Pendants

1 On a comfortable length of thread, pick up six 11º gold seed beads. Tie the 11ºs into a circle. Sew through the first 11º picked up again, and pull snug.

2 Work a right-angle weave increase stitch with 11ºs on each 11º picked up in step 1. The finished round will have 12 11ºs on the outer edge. Step up through the first 11º picked up to start the next round.

3 Work right-angle weave with 11ºs. Increase on every other 11º picked up in step 2. The finished round will have 18 11ºs. Step up to start the next round.

4 Work right-angle weave with 15º gold seed beads on every 11º picked up in step 3. The finished round will have 18 15ºs. Step up to start the next round.

5 Work right-angle weave with 15ºs on every 15º picked up in step 4. The finished round will have 18 15ºs. Step up to start the next round.

6 Center a 14mm rivoli in the beadwork. Sew through all the 15º up-beads, and pull snug around the 14mm. Sew through all the 15ºs in the round again and pull snug.

7 Work the needle to a 15º up-bead in one of the stitches in step 4 (the first round with 15ºs).

8 Sew a 15º between each 15º up-bead in this round. End the threads.

9 Repeat steps 1–8 three times for a total of four 14mm pendants **(photo a)**.

Make 16mm Rivoli Pendants

10 On a comfortable length of thread, pick up six 11ºs. Tie the 11ºs into a circle. Sew through the first 11º picked up again, and pull snug.

11 Work a right-angle weave increase stitch with 11ºs on each 11º picked up in step 10. The finished row will have 12 11ºs on the outer edge. Step up to start the next round.

12 Work right-angle weave with 11ºs. Increase on every other 11º picked up in step 11. The finished row will have 18 11ºs. Step up to start the next round.

13 Work right-angle weave with 15ºs. Increase on every third 11º picked up in step 12. The finished row will have 24 15ºs. Step up to start the next round.

14 Work right-angle weave with 15ºs on every 15º picked up in step 13. The finished round will have 24 15ºs. Step up to start the next round.

15 Work right-angle weave with 15ºs on every 15º picked up in step 14. The finished round will have 24 15ºs. Step up to start the next round.

16 Center a 16mm rivoli in the beadwork. Sew through all the 15º up-beads, and pull snug around the rivoli. Sew through all the 15ºs in the round again, pulling snug.

17 Work the needle to a 15º up- (or top) bead in one of the stitches in step 13. Since this was an increase round, every third stitch will have two 15ºs for the increase in the up-beads. Sew an 11º between each 15º in this round. The 11ºs will be a snug fit, so pull them into place carefully. End the threads.

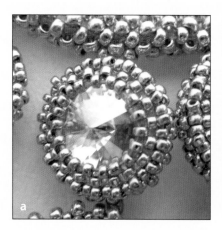

18 Repeat steps 10–17 three times for a total of four 16mm pendants **(photo b)**.

Make a 16mm Rivoli Center Pendant
19 Repeat steps 10–16.

20 Work the needle to a 15º up- (or top) bead picked up in step 14. This is the second round using 15ºs. Sew a 15º between each 15º in this round **(photo c)**.

Make an 18mm Rivoli Center Pendant
21 On a comfortable length of thread, pick up six 11ºs. Tie the 11ºs into a circle. Sew through the first 11º again, and pull snug.

22 Work a right-angle weave increase stitch with 11ºs on each 11º picked up in step 21. The finished row will have 12 11º on the outer edge. Step up to start the next round.

23 Work right-angle weave stitches with 11ºs. Increase on every other 11º picked up in step 22. The finished round will have 18 11ºs. Step up to start the next round.

24 Work right-angle weave stitches with 11ºs. Increase on every third 11º picked up in step 23. The finished round will have 24 11ºs. Step up to start the next round.

25 Work right-angle weave stitches with 15ºs on every 11º picked up in step 24. The finished round will have 24 15ºs. Step up to start the next round.

26 Repeat step 25.

27 Center an 18mm rivoli in the beadwork. Sew through all the 15º up-beads, and pull snug around the rivoli. Sew through all the 15ºs in the ring again. Pull snug.

28 Work the needle to an 11º up- (or top) bead in one of the stitches in step 24. Since this was an increase round, every third stitch will have two 11ºs for the increase in the up-beads. Sew an 11º between each 11º in this round. The beads going between the increase beads will be a snug fit, so pull them into place carefully.

29 Sew an 11º between each 11º picked up in step 28. Repeat the thread path in this round again to reinforce. End the threads **(photo d)**.

Make the Toggle and Loop Clasp
30 On a comfortable length of thread, pick up 10 11ºs. Work in flat peyote stitch for eight rows. Zip the ends together to make a tube.

31 Work the needle to the center of the tube. Make a short strip by working peyote stitch two 11ºs wide for five 11º on each side. Sew a split ring to the end of the strip.

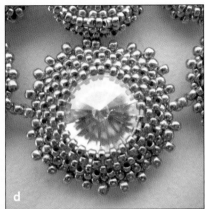

32 Pick up 22 11ºs. Sew through all the beads again in the same direction to make a loop. Repeat to reinforce.

33 Pick up two 11ºs, and sew through two beads on the loop. Sew a split ring to the two 11ºs just picked up.

Make the Necklace Rope

34 On a comfortable length of thread, work four flat right-angle weave stitches using 11ºs. Wrap the strip around the cord, and connect the ends with a fifth stitch.

35 Work in tubular right-angle weave for 17 in. (43cm).

36 Sew through the cord and rope several times to secure it. Trim the cord to fit inside the rope.

37 Sew through all the end 11ºs on the rope twice, and pull snug. Pick up three 11ºs. Sew through a split ring attached to a clasp half and an 11º on the opposite side of the rope. Reinforce.

38 Repeat steps 36–37 on the other end of the rope to attach the other half of the clasp.

Assemble the Necklace

39 Attach a new length of thread to a 14mm rivoli pendant. Using the 11ºs on the edges of the completed rivolis, sew the 14mm and 16mm rivoli pendants together in pairs.

40 Sew the 16mm rivoli center pendant to the 18mm rivoli center pendant in the same manner.

41 Locate the center of the rope, and sew the center pendant grouping from step 40 to an 11º in the rope.

42 Sew the pendant groupings from step 39 to the rope, spaced five stitches apart on on each side of the center pendant grouping.

43 As the pendants have a tendency to overlap slightly, place an 11º between the lower pendants on each pendant grouping to separate them: Locate a center 11º edge bead on a pendant. Match to a corresponding 11º on an adjacent pendant. Sew an 11º between the two pendants, using a ladder-type stitch. Repeat for each pair of pendants.

EARRINGS

1 For each earring drop: Follow the necklace steps 1–8 and 10–17.

2 Using an 11º on the edge of each rivoli pendant, sew a 14mm and a 16mm rivioli pendant together.

3 Make a small loop of four or five 15ºs at the other end of the 14mm rivoli pendant. Use a jump ring to attach an earring drop to an earring finding.

BASICS
Tools & Stitches

TOOLS FOR BEADING

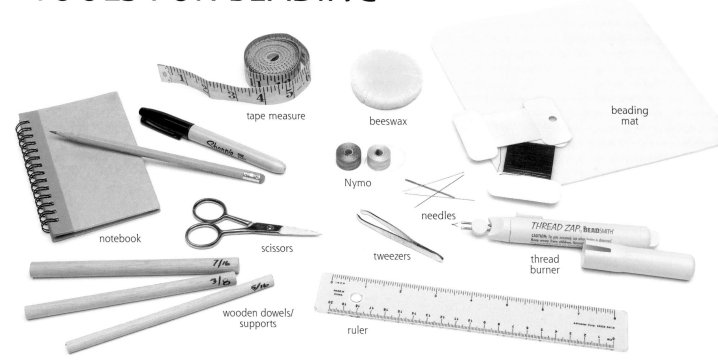

tape measure

beeswax

beading mat

notebook

Nymo

needles

scissors

tweezers

thread burner

wooden dowels/ supports

ruler

To complete the projects in this book, you'll need a few basic tools (most pictured above).

Needles: I normally use size 10 beading needles, about 2-in. (5cm) long. Size 12 beading needles are preferable when you are making many passes through a bead or the bead holes are small. A beading sharp, a needle about 1¼-in. (3.2cm) long, is useful for beading in tight corners.

Scissors: Use a very small, sharp pair only for nylon threads. Use another pair to cut Fireline and similar threads.

Beading thread: For most of the projects in this book, I used Nymo D thread in light and dark gold, bronze-brown, and black. Nymo is a parallel filament thread that is durable and flexible. A good substitute for Nymo is One-G.

Fireline: When I'm working with crystals, bugle, or metal beads which may have sharp edges, I prefer to use Fireline, a gel-spun polyethylene (GSP) thread, in either a 6# or 8# weight and in the smoke color.

Beading wire: This is a flexible wire made of steel wires twisted or braided together and coated with nylon used for stringing beads and components. I use .015–.019 in silver, gold, and bronze colors.

Thread burner: This battery-operated device heats up quickly. It cuts and seals nylon threads and gets rid of short ends and fuzz.

Thread conditioners: I normally don't condition thread, but you can use beeswax or Thread Heaven, a silicon-based product that helps prevent fraying, strengthens the thread, creates a slick coating, and imparts a slight static charge to reduce tangling.

Tweezers: Use a flat-tipped pair for pulling needles through beads and a pointy tipped pair for undoing tangles and knots.

Ruler: A 6-in. (15cm) one fits in the toolbox. A cloth tape measure is handy.

Bead scoop: This is a long, narrow, curved piece of metal used to pick up beads or rearrange them on the bead mat. A triangle sorter also works well.

Wooden dowels (supports): Use dowels about 6 in. (15cm) long of various diameters as supports for tubular beading.

Beading mat or surface: I use Vellux pads, readily available from bead stores, in a light beige or ivory color.

Pliers and cutters: Choose a good pair of chainnose pliers, either straight or curved, roundnose pliers, crimping pliers, and a flush wire cutter.

STITCH BASICS

Flat Peyote Stitch

Even-Count Flat Peyote Stitch

1 Pick up a stop bead (p. 94) and sew through it again.

2 Pick up an even number of beads (10 here). These beads become the first and second rows.

3 Pick up a bead **(figure, bead 11)**, and sew back through the next-to-last bead picked up in step 2 **(bead 9)**. The new bead will sit on top of the last bead of the first row **(bead 10)**.

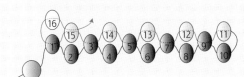

4 Pick up a bead **(bead 12)**, skip a bead **(bead 8)**, and sew through the next bead **(bead 7)**. Notice how the new bead pushes the bead below it down about a half bead, creating the characteristic up/down of peyote stitch.

5 Pick up a bead **(bead 13)**, skip a bead **(bead 6)**, and sew through the next bead **(bead 5)**.

6 Continue picking up a bead, skipping a bead, and sewing through the next bead to the end of the row.

7 To start the next row, pick up a bead **(bead 16)** and sew through the up-bead **(bead 15)** on the previous row.

8 Continue across the row, placing a new bead between each up-bead.

9 Repeat steps 6–8 for the length of the piece.

10 When you finish with the beadwork, remove the stop bead.

Odd-Count Flat Peyote

Odd-count flat peyote lets you make designs that are centered. However, every other row requires a special turning technique. Here are two ways to make the turn. I describe five more ways in my book, *Bead Tube Jewelry*.

Woven Turn (Figure-8 Turn)

Pick up the first two rows and work the third row as you would for even-count peyote stitch. Just before the end of the row **(figure, exiting bead e)**:

1 Sew through the last beads **(beads a and b)** in the previous rows.

2 Pick up the last bead **(bead c)** for the current row.

3 Sew through two beads **(beads a and d)** in the previous rows.

4 Sew through the bead **(bead e)** directly above the last bead exited **(bead d)** and through two beads **(beads a and b)** in the previous rows.

If the ends of the beadwork do not match up properly, you may need one more row of peyote.

5 Sew through the last bead picked up **(bead c)**, and continue in peyote stitch back across the row.

Looped Turn

Work two rows in peyote stitch. At the end of the row, for the first turn:

1 Pick up the last bead of the row.

2 Tie the tail thread and working thread together.

3 Sew back through the last bead picked up and continue in peyote stitch across the row. You can also work a woven turn for the first row.

For subsequent turns:

1 Pick up the last bead of the row **(figure, bead a)**.

2 Pass the needle under the loop of thread connecting the end beads of the two previous rows.

3 Sew back through the last bead picked up **(bead a)** and continue in peyote stitch across the row.

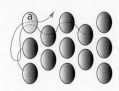

STITCH BASICS

Tubular Peyote Stitch

Even-Count Tubular Peyote Stitch

Even-count tubular peyote makes horizontal rings around the tube. Each round shifts one bead to the left from the previous round and requires a step-up to start each new round.

1 Pick up an even number of beads and tie the beads into a circle.

2 Sew through the bead to the left of the knot **(figure, bead a)**, and begin picking up beads as you would for flat peyote: Pick up a bead, skip a bead, and sew through the next bead.

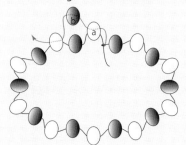

3 Each time a round ends, sew through the last bead of the previous round **(bead a)** and the first bead of the current round **(bead b)**. This is the step-up.

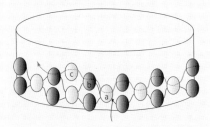

4 Pick up a bead **(bead c)**, and continue filling between the up-beads for the length desired.

Odd-Count Tubular Peyote Stitch

Odd-count tubular peyote produces a continuous spiral. It does not require a step-up.

1 Pick up an odd number of beads and tie the beads into a circle. Use a support, like a pen or dowel, if needed.

2 Sew through the bead to the left of the knot and begin picking up beads as you would for flat peyote: Pick up a bead, skip a bead, and sew through the next bead.

3 Work continuously around the tube, filling between the up-beads for the length desired.

Zipping Up

To make a tube or a bangle bracelet, you'll need to join up the ends of flat peyote beadwork. Fortunately, peyote has a natural up-down sequence that makes zipping it together easy.

Match up the ends, like a little zipper, and sew through the beads, zigzagging from top to bottom through the up-beads and pulling the edges together snugly. End the thread in the beadwork. If there is a tail thread, work it into the beadwork also, or use it to reinforce the join.

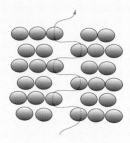

Ladder Stitch

Start a ladder of beads by picking up two beads. Slide the beads near the end of the thread. Sew through the first bead again in the same direction. Position the two beads so they lie flat, side-by-side. Sew through the second bead. Continue by picking up one bead and sewing back through the previous bead and the bead just picked up for the length desired. Notice that the direction of the thread loop between the beads changes direction each time, from clockwise to counterclockwise, and back again. Each bead is one "rung" of the ladder.

Two-Drop Ladder Stitch

Start a two-drop ladder of beads by picking up four beads. Slide the beads near the end of the thread. Sew through the first two beads again in the same direction. Position the four beads so they sit side-by-side in two stacks of two. Sew through the second set of beads. Continue by picking up two beads and sewing through the previous bead stack and the two-bead stack just picked up for the length desired. Now you have two beads in each rung of the ladder.

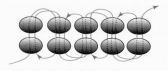

Brick Stitch

Flat Brick Stitch

1 Make a ladder of beads the length desired (see Ladder Stitch, p. 90).

2 Start the next row by picking up two beads. Pass the needle under the loop of thread connecting the last two beads on the previous row (the thread bridge). Settle the new beads parallel to the previous row and side-by-side with each other. Sew back up through the second (inside) bead of the pair.

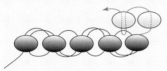

3 Continue the row by picking up one bead, looping under the thread bridge between the next pair of beads on the previous row, and sewing back up through the new bead. Repeat to the end of the row.

4 Repeat steps 2 and 3 for the length of the piece.

Tubular Brick Stitch

1 Make a ladder the length needed.

2 Connect the beginning and ending beads of the ladder by sewing through both beads. Be careful not to twist the ladder.

2 Position the circle of beads so the thread is exiting upward by turning the bead circle over or sewing through one of the beads to position the thread.

4 Follow steps 2 and 3 in the Flat Brick Stitch instructions to make the next round.

5 At the end of the round, connect the beginning and ending beads by sewing through the first bead of the round. Loop under the thread bridge below it, and sew back through the same bead.

6 Repeat steps 4 and 5 for the length of the tube.

Tubular Herringbone Stitch

1 Pick up an even number of beads. Tie the beads into a circle.

2 Sew through the first bead picked up. Pick up two beads, and sew through the next two beads. Continue around the circle, picking up two beads and sewing through two beads each time, to complete the round.

3 To step up to the next round, sew through the first bead in the previous round plus the first bead picked up in the current round. Pick up two beads to start the new round. Sew through the next two beads of the previous round. Repeat to finish the round.

Square Stitch

1 Pick up the first bead of the first row of your pattern. Slide the bead near the end of the thread. Sew through the bead again in the same direction. This acts as both your first bead and as a stop bead so the rest of the beads won't slide off. Pick up the rest of the beads for the first row.

2 Pick up a bead. Sew through the bead right below on the first row, and sew through the new bead again. Repeat across the row.

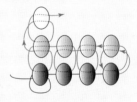

3 Start a new row by picking up a bead and sewing through the bead on the previous row and through the new bead again. Repeat steps 2 and 3 for the desired length.

> To stabilize and strengthen square stitch, when you finish a row, sew through all the beads on the previous row and then through all the beads on the current row again before starting the next row.

STITCH BASICS

Right-Angle Weave Stitch

Flat Right-Angle Weave

1 Pick up four beads, and tie them into a circle (or sew through all the beads again). Position the thread tail to the left of the top bead. Exit the right side bead.

2 Pick up three beads. Sew through the bead exited at the start of this step and the next two beads.

3 Pick up three beads. Sew through the bead exited at the start of this step and the next two beads.

4 To start the next row, sew through the bottom bead of the last stitch. Pick up three beads, and sew through the bead exited at the start of this step and the next bead.

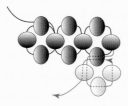

5 Pick up two beads, and sew through the bottom bead of the stitch directly above. Continue through the next three beads of this stitch and the bottom bead of the stitch to the above left.

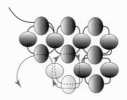

6 Complete the last stitch and position your thread to exit the bottom bead of the new stitch.

Things to Remember About Right-Angle Weave

In the beginning row, the first stitch requires four beads. Each stitch after the first one in the beginning row requires three beads. The first stitch of every new row also requires three beads. Every subsequent stitch in the row requires only two beads. At the end of the row, position your needle so it exits the bottom bead of the row just completed.

Each stitch in right-angle weave changes direction from clockwise to counterclockwise. Many people see this as "making figure-8s." The thread never crosses horizontally or vertically from one bead to the next. It always makes a right-angle turn.

By positioning your thread tail to the left of the top bead in the first stitch, you can always reorient your beadwork and figure out which direction the next stitch goes.

Count right-angle weave stitches by counting the beads on the edge.

Tubular Right-Angle Weave

1 Work a strip of flat right-angle weave the circumference desired, minus one stitch.

2 Join the ends of the strip by picking up a bead, sewing through the side bead on the other end of the strip, picking up a bead, and sewing back through the starting bead.

3 Continue sewing through beads to position the thread in an edge bead. Begin the next round with three beads. Continue stitching around the circle, alternating stitch direction. Each stitch will require two beads. Only one bead is required to complete the last stitch and join the ends of the round.

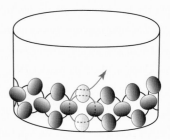

4 Repeat step 3 for the length desired.

Circular Right-Angle Weave Stitch

Several projects use circular right-angle weave to encase cabochons or rivolis. These are general directions and diagrams for the first four rows. Read the instructions for each project carefully, as there may be fewer rows or more rows, or bead sizes may change.

While each stitch alternates direction from clockwise to counterclockwise as it always does in right-angle weave, I work in a clockwise direction in circular right-angle weave. The start of each row in the diagrams is marked with a blue star.

Row 1: Pick up six beads and tie them into a circle.

Row 2: A right-angle weave increase stitch is worked on each bead on row 1. An increase stitch has five total beads instead of the normal four beads. The first stitch requires four new beads; each subsequent stitch needs three beads, and the last stitch of the row only two.

Exiting the left side of the first bead, pick up four beads. Work the stitch clockwise, and sew through the next bead to the right on row 1. Stitches 2–5 require three beads each.

Alternate the direction of each stitch. The last stitch requires only two beads to complete the row. Use the diagram to position your thread to start the next row. Stop and count the beads on the outside edge of the beadwork. There should be 12 **(figure 1)**.

Row 3: Make increases in every other stitch: Starting with the first increase bead of the first stitch on row 2, work a normal stitch on the first bead and an increase stitch on the second bead.

The first stitch is worked counterclockwise from the right side of the start bead and requires three beads. The second stitch also requires three beads. After that, the stitches alternate between normal stitches requiring two beads and increase stitches requiring three beads. The last stitch requires only two beads. Use the diagram to position your thread to start the next row. Stop and count the beads on the outside edge of the beadwork. There

It is very important to stop after each row. Count the beads on the outside edge of the beadwork to be sure you have the correct number of stitches and beads. Straighten the beads so you can see them easily for the next row. The circle of beads tends to be irregular while you work.

should be 18 **(figure 2)**.

Row 4: Make increases in every third stitch: Starting in the first increase bead of the twelfth stitch in row 3, work normal stitches on the two increase stitches on row 3 and an increase stitch on each of the normal stitches on row 3.

The first stitch is worked counterclockwise from the right side of the start bead and requires three beads. The second stitch requires only two beads for a normal stitch. The third stitch is an increase and requires three beads. Continue beading, alternating stitch direction, working a normal stitch on each increase stitch bead of row 3 and an increase stitch on each normal stitch in row 3. The last stitch requires only two beads. Stop and count the beads on the outside edge of the beadwork. There should be 24 **(figure 3)**.

figure 1

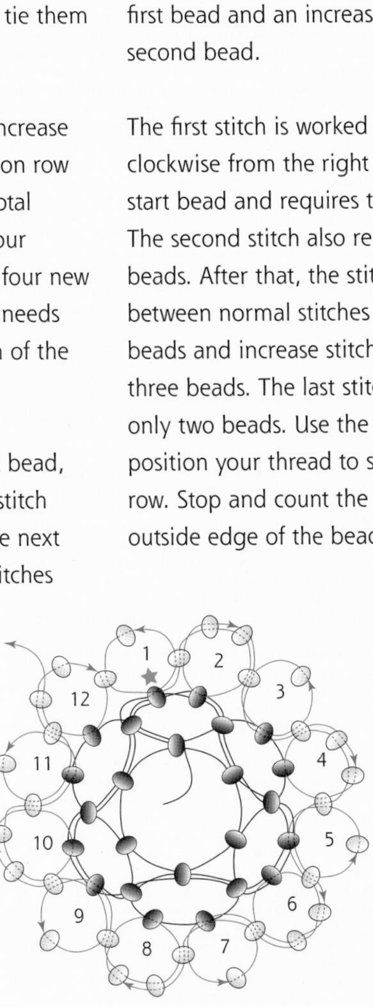

figure 2

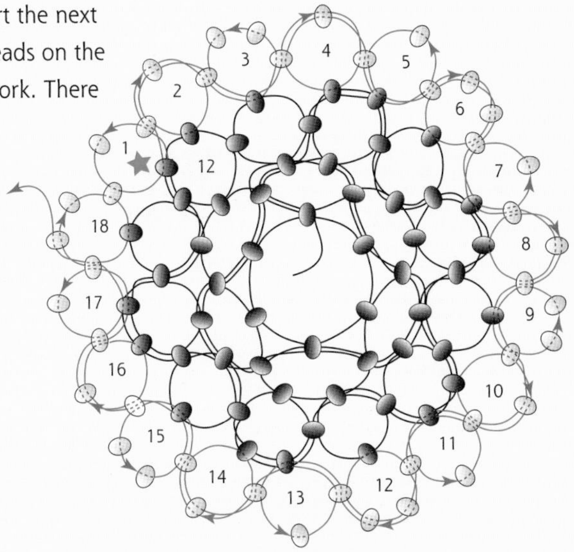

figure 3

STITCH BASICS

St. Petersburg Chain Stitch

Accent beads may be a different color or size.

1 Slide a stop bead near the end of the thread, leaving a 6-in. (15cm) tail.

2 Pick up six beads. Slide the beads down to the stop bead. Sew through the third and fourth beads again, pulling the last two beads parallel to them **(figure 1)**.

3 Pick up a bead (accent bead) and sew through three beads directly below it **(figure 2)**.

4 Pick up a bead (accent bead) and sew through the two beads above it **(figure 3)**.

5 Pick up four beads and sew through the first two again in the same direction, pulling the last two beads parallel **(figure 4)**.

6 Pick up a bead (accent bead) and sew through the three beads directly below it **(figure 5)**.

7 Pick up a bead (accent bead) and sew through the two beads above it **(figure 6)**.

8 Repeat steps 5–7 for the length of the beadwork.

Stop Bead

A stop bead is used to keep other beads on the thread while starting a piece of beadwork and to provide some resistance while working the first row. A stop bead is any bead that is a different color, shape or size than those in the beadwork.

Pick up the stop bead, slide it near the end of the thread, and sew through the stop bead again in the same direction. The loop of thread around the bead holds it in place, while allowing you to slide the bead up and down the thread. When you no longer need the stop bead, slide it off the tail of the thread and secure the tail in the beadwork.

Beginning and Ending Threads

To end a thread, weave back into the beadwork, following the existing thread path and tying two or three half-hitch knots around the thread between beads as you go. Change direction as you weave so the thread crosses itself. Sew through a few beads after the last knot before cutting the thread. To begin a new thread, start several rows below the ending point and weave through the beadwork, tying half-hitch knots between beads and exiting the last bead picked up. Trim the tail of the new thread close to the beadwork.

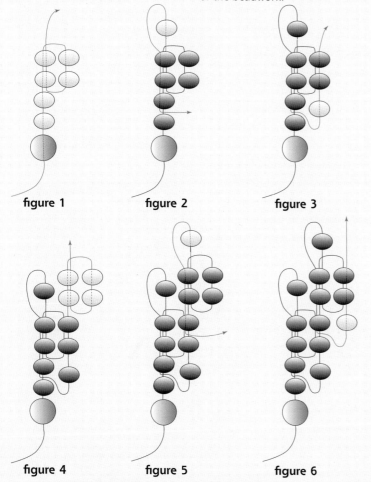

figure 1   figure 2   figure 3

figure 4   figure 5   figure 6

Half-Hitch Knot

Use a half-hitch knot to secure the thread when starting or ending a thread. It is also useful to secure the thread as you are working to maintain tension or to provide a stop in case a thread breaks in the beadwork.

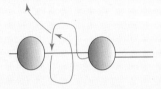

Sew under a thread between two beads, forming a small loop above the thread. Sew back through the loop, and pull to draw the knot down between the beads.

Overhand Knot

Make a loop at the end of the thread. Pull the tail end through the loop and tighten. If working with doubled thread, make the loop with both threads and pull both tail ends through the loop.

Square Knot

Bring the left-hand thread over the right-hand thread and then bring it under and back up on top.

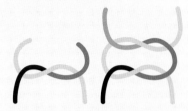

Next, cross the right-hand thread over the left-hand thread, then under it and back up over the top of the thread. Pull both the threads to tighten the knot.

ABOUT THE AUTHOR

Nancy Zellers is a designer and writer who truly enjoys creating amazing beadwork, one bead at a time. She takes seed beads and turns them into something different, bigger, and totally unexpected using her analytical perspective and software design training.

Her first exposure to beadwork was in the '70s, when she explored loomed beadwork and needlepoint. In the '90s, she took several art classes and started producing sculptural works with seed beads. These sculptures have appeared in over 28 local and national contemporary art exhibitions.

Nancy acquired new techniques and expanded her view of the bead world through classes with many leading beadwork teachers. Branching out of the solitary artist's studio, she began designing jewelry pieces and developing instructional material. She has published more than 35 articles in magazines and books. Her first book, *Bead Tube Jewelry*, was published by Kalmbach Books in 2011. She has been teaching on the local and national level for more than 10 years.

Nancy designs beadwork that is very wearable, and she loves strong colors and clean lines. She can usually be found in her hot-pink-and-lime-green studio in Denver, sewing one little bead to another little bead. Contact Nancy at *nzbeads.com*.

Bead Tube Jewelry

Peyote & brick stitch designs for
30+ necklaces, bracelets, and earrings

Nancy Zellers

64179 • $19.95

More beading fun from Nancy Zellers!

Discover how one little bead tube can create many different looks! Artist and author Nancy Zellers takes it to the limit with this utterly original book. You'll enjoy the easy-to-read patterns for each tube and the project instructions that incorporate them into a multitude of jewelry styles, from casual, informal designs to metallic, dressy pieces.

- Create 30+ designs using peyote and brick stitch

- Fashion colorful seed beads into jewelry ranging from funky to elegant

- Stitch tubes easily by following clear, color-coded patterns